KARL MOORE

THE SECRET ART OF SELF-DEVELOPMENT

16 little-known rules for eternal happiness & freedom

Inspire3 Publishing
20-22 Wenlock Road
London, N1 7GU

www.inspire3.com

eISBN 978-0-9559935-0-3

WHAT INDUSTRY LEADERS ARE SAYING ABOUT THIS BOOK

"We are in the midst of one of the greatest paradigm shifts in history. We clearly need a new direction on how we think. Our old models do not work any longer. If you are looking to make a quantum shift in your thinking towards more freedom and less suffering, Karl Moore delivers with this new book an outstanding piece of information. It is down to earth, profound in is clarity, and simple in its understanding. A must read."
– *Thomas Herold, www.dreammanifesto.com*

"This book may shock you a little and it will certainly 'wake you up' and get you moving in a very positive direction. Written in an easy to read and understand style, it gets right to the heart of self-development. You will start looking at life with your eyes wide open today... and you will LOVE it! Congratulations to you, Karl, for being the brave, bold pioneer that you are!"
– *Rebecca Marina, www.rebeccamarina.com*

"I have not been able to put down this book. Each chapter is better than the one before. It's made me see the world around me in a whole new light. Amazing book, and I recommend it for everyone who is seeking to find their own road map to self-development and true inner happiness."
- *J. Walker, www.natural-life-choices.com*

"This is a wholeheartedly enjoyable and enlightening read, seemingly simple, yet positively profound. Karl's book effortlessly tackles topics such as taking responsibility, letting go, overcoming, intention, accepting change, and being truly happy. Karl debunks many self-help myths and illuminates deep themes in a straightforward and often light-hearted way and I love the easy to follow exercises and will carry on using them in my day-to-day life - highly recommended!! "
– *Johnny London, www.affirmationstation.com*

"I found myself nodding as I read this book, as if some deeper part of me had known this material all along yet was unable to grasp the ease of which it could be applied. Thank you Karl for introducing me to a whole new part of myself and unleashing the power that I have within. This book takes the best secrets from all areas of self development and packs them into one easy read. "
- *John Derrick, www.johnderrick.com*

"This book is a guide to finding your own path to self-fulfilment - and not just blindly following the latest fad or guru. That's just one of the teachings I learned from this book. People are all different (even weird!), so there is no one 'true way' that fits everybody."
- *Chris Lloyd, www.ultrabraintraining.com*

"I've just finished reading this book - and highly recommend you do the same. It says more in 150 pages than most do in 15,000. Rules are clearly stated and explained so that you can put them into practice immediately and best of all - simply."
- *Dick Ingersoll, www.applying-the-law-of-attraction.com*

"Self improvement, I have found, unfolds beautifully all on it's own - if you let it. Karl Moore has taken Occam's razor to the whole business of self-development and delivers it how it's supposed to be: simple and practical. The realizations in this book are powerful for that reason and will undoubtedly resonate with many, many 'seekers'. If only this book had come into my life years ago! Excellent job, Karl!"
- *Daniel Topp, www.vastwellnesscenter.com*

"To say that Karl's writing lights my fire is an understatement! I read his Happiness book back to back - after which my energy was simply buzzing. This book is even better! This is spiritual food for the soul; feed regularly and you will become nourished with fulfilment in your life. Your thirst will be sated, your heart will sing with joy and your soul will reach a peace only once before thought impossible. I believe there is a time for everything and everything has it's time: and it is time for you to read The Secret Art Of Self–Development. Thank you Karl - it will be beside my bed from now on!"
- *Valery Coburn, www.inspirationplus.net*

"I always thought that the trouble with life, is that it doesn't come with a manual. This book fixes that problem. It's the most practical, inspirational, and easy to read 'user guide' for life I've ever found. This book is bad news for expensive self help gurus; everything you need to know about being happy and successful is distilled into these pages."
- *Harvey Walsh, www.daytradingfreedom.com*

"Searching for a better life? Look no further than this book. Karl Moore opens the door to your freedom, happiness and success, offering easily accessible guidance in a friendly conversational tone. Forget all the jargon and typical nonsense that often surrounds personal growth. Karl helps you find empowerment to live the life you want. This book is, without doubt, a total revelation and the only guide you'll need for your self-development journey. Absolutely brilliant!"
- *Carol Anne Strange, www.carolannestrange.com*

"Thanks to Karl Moore my income has grown 1,200% in two years. Karl has now come out with the secrets to his success. If you're looking for happiness in your life, I highly recommend this book. I've known Karl for years – and this is the only guide you'll ever need for finding true happiness in your life."
- *Mark Anastasi, www.mark-anastasi.com*

"What a great book! A very succinct and easy to understand guide to happiness. I always knew that everyone could experience happiness in the moment – and Karl's book shows you how. Happiness come from within and this book shows you how to find it."
- *Will Thomas, www.tampabaydogwhisperer.com*

"The more fundamental a truth, the simpler it is. We search for answers in complex theories and yet if we throw away our blinkers, the truth is staring us in the face. The 'blinkers' are limiting beliefs and false preconceptions: the things 'everybody knows' that are simply wrong. This easy to understand manual explains how you can get back in touch with what simply 'is' - and then all things become possible."
- Peter Shepherd, www.trans4mind.com

"Karl is one of the most spiritual people I know. He's known in the industry as the Bubbling Buddha, and I highly recommend his work."
– David Riklan, www.selfgrowth.com

"My 13 year old daughter once mentioned that life was effortless. It was a word that stuck with me. I relished it. Effortless. And it can be. Life can be effortless. Sometimes we need a helping hand to remember how to make it so and this book is a fantastic place to start. In a series of easy-to-read pep talks in the author's delightfully fresh and down to earth style, Karl becomes the friend you always need when the going gets tough. He's the type of real friend who doesn't collude with your stuff, but asks you to simply step into your personal best, and shows you how. An excellent book for any seeker who, as Karl puts it, wants to become a finder. Wonderful!"
- Billie Dean, www.billiedean.com

"We all want happiness, rich relationships, abundant and fulfilling lives, vibrant health and a winning mindset. The access to all these gifts is available to us for the asking if we are willing to commit to the path of personal development and allow each day to provide us with countless opportunities for developing our inner wisdom,

the potential for maximizing our personal effectivess and the art of manifesting our dream lives intentionally. This book is an insightful guide to uncovering your inner guru and discovering what it takes to lead your best life. If you want to be your best and are ready to live a life without limits, read this book"
– *Dr. Joe Rubino, www.centerforpersonalreinvention.com*

"This book offers concise yet fully explained 'rules' to make one's life free and happy. I love it's non-linear organization. I can pick it up and flip to any chapter and be inspired, encouraged, uplifted and guided towards a better tomorrow. Thank you Karl!"
– *Mark McCoid, www.healingproducts.com*

"Why is success so hard? There are thousands of self-help websites, books, courses, retreats, CDs and videos dealing with the subject and we still search and search for self-development. Well, that's a good thing, but it doesn't have to be hard. In fact, it can be pretty easy when you're holding a book like this one. There are no 10 steps to follow, no lists to write, no mountain to climb... just a way to 'be' and Karl shows just how it's done... easily."
- *Tom Murasso, www.borntomanifest.com*

"I love that this book hits the nail on the head, talking about areas of life that when focused on positively will indeed turn your life around. Karl reminds us that change is constant, and it is not to be feared. That YOU are in the driving set so consciously set your intentions, as your life is a reflection of where your focus is. And that happiness is a choice that is available to everyone. If you struggle to believe that, then you MUST read his book, as you will be convinced and more by the end of it!"
- *Arabella Jolie, www.whyte-witch.com*

"The aim of self-development is to recognise who we truly are, and how we've always been free of all that constrains our creativity and happiness. Karl Moore has given us a straight-forward guide to achieving that. He delivers 16 life-changing steps on this re-evolutionary path - which we can each begin to take today."
- *Johnathan Brooks, www.spiritbearcoaching.com*

"I read this book all through in one sitting - then went back to the start and read it all again. Like all great teachers, Karl Moore has the knack of explaining sometimes complex ideas in a way that is not just understandable but actually enjoyable. The Secret Art of Self-Development is essential reading for anyone who wants to get more out of life both materially and spiritually."
- *Nick Daws, www.mywritingblog.com*

"Excellent book! If you're looking to find your freedom, then this book will take you there. Karl distils the best self-development wisdom around into a simple, easy-to-understand format. He even talks about my favourite topic – releasing. If you're looking for self-development, stop right here!"
– *Larry Crane, www.releasetechnique.com*

"Karl Moore did it again! This book is written for those of us who long for learning and search after the power to awaken our greatest passions and deepest aspirations. The book is humorous, filled with linguistic extravagance, sheer inventiveness and deep insights – with simple yet profound delivery."
– *Evane Abbassi, www.alternatedisputeresolutioninc.com*

"Karl uses a simplistic style to pull back the curtain and expose what happiness and self-development are truly all about. Forget all the self-help hype - You will learn how easy it can be to accept, let go and move on to a happier, more fulfilling life. Great read Karl, thanks!"
- *Gene Anger, www.best-self-help-sites.com*

"I have known and have had the pleasure of working with Karl for about four years now within the self-development arena. I must tell you that if there are significantly more genuine and more inspiring individuals in this field today I haven't met them... and let me tell you I've met just about everybody. It's no accident that he was hand selected as one of the 12 key teachers in The Meta Secret movie and the reasoning for which is 100% clear within only a few seconds of reading this book. Karl is a true visionary and I'm very thankful to call him a friend."
- *Joe DePalma, www.readysetrise.com*

ABOUT THE AUTHOR

Karl Moore is an entrepreneur and self-development leader.

He has spent over 15 years exploring the world of personal improvement, and is a featured teacher from the movie *Think*.

Karl is the author of six best-selling books, including *The Secret Art of Self-Development*.

You can visit Karl's official website at www.karlmoore.com.

"The aim of life is self-development. To realize one's nature perfectly – that is what each of us is here for."

– Oscar Wilde

CONTENTS

Foreword By Dr Mel Gill 1

Introduction 5

The Ultimate Truth 7

How To Use This Book 11

Rule #1: Stop Feeling Sorry For Yourself! 13

Rule #2: Learn To Let Go 17

Rule #3: Your Brain Is Limiting You 22

Rule #4: Stop Being So Damn Sensitive 27

Rule #5: Be Happy Now 31

Rule #6: Release Your Religion 36

Rule #7: Intention Sets Direction 41

Rule #8: Say Yes More 45

Rule #9: Change Is The Only Constant 49

Rule #10: People Are Weird. Love Them For It 53

Rule #11: You Can't Change The Past 58

Rule #12: Fill Your Life With Happiness 63

Rule #13: Be A Rich Monk! 68

Rule #14: Sadness Is Okay. It's All Good.................................73

Rule #15: You Are Not Your Story...77

Rule #16: Smile, Laugh, Love Yourself! 82

The Secret Art of Self-Development Review 86

Conclusion 90

Appendix 1: A Short Course In Releasing 95

Appendix 2: Quotes To Inspire..106

Appendix 3: Experiences To Open Your Eyes Again!..........111

Appendix 4: Foods To Make You Happy 115

Appendix 5: Songs To Make You Smile 118

Appendix 6: Claim Your Free MP3 Version of This Book...121

FOREWORD
BY DR MEL GILL

Self-development in its truest form is a desire for freedom.

The freedom to express one's self from a vital core that pulsates with every authentic fiber of being.

It's an inner urge to truly understand yourself, and how you contribute to the world around you. It's a yearning to break through self-imposed limitations and self-sabotage. It's a search for truth.

Your truth.

We all begin this journey from the moment of birth.

But there are a few who are more than half-way through that spiritual voyage towards enlightenment. They are more aware, more mindful, more connected to the source and seem to attract EXACTLY what they need for personal growth.

You're one of them.

Let me share something with you.

In the course of doing what comes naturally to me, teaching people what I know, I've been recognized as the world's #1 motivational speaker by some of the largest media groups in the business. I've been heavily featured on TV and radio, and currently run a number of multi-million dollar corporations.

As director of *The Meta Secret*, I've also worked with some of the most successful, most spiritually-realized individuals in the world.

They each know universal secrets that would blow you away.

But there was one gentleman that stood out above the crowd of people I meet daily.

I remember that it was his energy, his drive and his vision that held my attention. He had a clarity of purpose that belied his age. One that some would call an Old Soul, his was the voice of a guide to Higher Knowledge.

And you're holding his book.

Karl Moore has become known in the industry as the "Bubbling Buddha." He's a wonderfully happy guy – and a tremendously successful businessman. In his own life, he's combined spirituality and personal growth, with absolutely outstanding results.

He knows self-development from its core.

Accurately and with joy, Karl points the way to freedom, and happiness, and success for all his fellow beings.

In this book, he's taken out the hype – and distilled the wisdom of almost every philosopher and self-development course out there. And he's simplified it in a way that anyone can understand.

So, if you're looking for a breakthrough in your personal freedom... If you're looking to enjoy more success in all areas of your life... If you're looking to become self-developed...

Then sit back, and let Karl Moore show you the way.

I know you'll enjoy the ride.

Dr Mel Gill
Director, The Meta Secret
www.DrMelGill.com

INTRODUCTION

Self-development is a glorious quest.

It's the desire to find your own freedom. To connect with your own sense of worth, and integrity, and happiness. To enjoy abundance.

But for most people, self-development remains just that.

A quest. A journey. They never reach that point of realization, when all of the pieces fit together and they can finally stop "seeking."

They watched *What the Bleep* and *The Secret*. They attended the overseas holistic healing workshops. They bought the costly four-digit CD courses. They continued seeking, but they never found.

Their quest was honorable – and yet the search for self-development, the desire for freedom, was left unsatisfied.

This book is where the journey ends.

It's a simple collection of 16 "pep talks" to help you reconnect with your own true freedom, and to remove all of the crazy "rules" that you've built up so far during your journey.

It's a book that will blast through your own self-limitations, and break down any imaginary walls that are stopping you achieving greatness. It'll clear the grey clouds in your world, and show you the sun that was always shining just behind them.

This commonsense book will reconnect you with your own spirituality, your happiness, and your wonder for the world. That's my promise.

The self-development world is crammed full of *seekers*.

You, however, are about to become a *finder*.

So, read on, and enjoy!

Karl Moore,
www.karlmoore.com

THE ULTIMATE TRUTH

*"There is nothing either bad or good. Only
thinking makes it so." – William Shakespeare*

Would you like to enjoy TRUE FREEDOM?

To be free of emotional addictions… of desperately wanting
approval… of the feeling that you're broken… free of your
troublesome past… of your lack of abundance… free of stress
and worry… of limitations…

To feel in harmony with everything in your life. To smile, and
laugh, and love, while knowing that everything is happening
just as it should. To throw away all the rules. To be truly happy.

Doesn't that sound ideal?

**This book is about guiding you toward experiencing that
freedom.**

We're not experiencing true freedom right now, because we're surrounded by limitation.

Our brains limit us, reminding us of our bad habits, telling us that we can't achieve the things we desire. Our personality limits us, demanding that we seek approval, ensuring that we get stressed over the smallest of detail. Our religions limit us, forcing us to live by a set of rules that often conflict with our own thoughts.

We each build up our worlds around a particular set of beliefs, a set of rules, then fight against them, tripping ourselves up along the way.

The truth is that no belief system can grant true freedom.

Every single belief is limiting.

From personal beliefs about yourself, to the rules found in self-help books, to the policies of the big religions. Every "system" only provides a fresh set of limitations to hold you back. Limitations which come from nowhere and mean nothing.

This book is about removing those limitations.

It's about realizing that freedom comes from inside. It's about letting go of the limiting thoughts that have held you back in your life so far, so that you can discover your own true happiness.

The 16 "rules" aren't even really rules. They're just pointers to help you gradually realize and dig out the handful of limiting thoughts that are currently restricting how you live your life.

Limiting thoughts turn singers into accountants. Limiting thoughts force gay people into straight marriages. Limiting thoughts ensure drug addicts continue their addiction. Limiting thoughts make people desperately cling to the past, unable to move forward with life. Limiting thoughts stop us from doing the things we've always wanted – and loving ourselves for it. We feel bound by our labels.

Yes – Limiting thoughts LIMIT US.

Let go of all limiting thoughts – and you will experience true freedom, true self-development, true happiness.

And that is the ultimate truth, the meta-theme behind this book.

Each of us is already whole and complete and free and "self-developed." We're only limited by the thoughts we hold in mind.

If you wish, you can close this book right now, put it down, and get on with life. You already know everything you need to.

But if you feel you need to continue, then I'd be honored to be your guide.

The 16 "pep talks" which follow are each intended to guide you back to freedom, slowly releasing the most common limiting thoughts that bind most of us.

Each rule contains profound realizations if you choose to look close enough.

You'll be asked questions along the way, to help you decide for yourself which limiting thoughts you'd like to let go of, and which you'd like to keep.

In short, what follows is a simple reminder of genuine freedom – and the easy steps we can each take to rediscover it.

So, if you'd like to – smile, and continue reading.

How To Use This Book

This book contains 16 simple "rules" for helping you uncover common limitations, and discover your own true freedom and happiness.

It's easy to read, and simple to use. (Because self-development doesn't have to be hard work.)

You can read this book in the traditional way. Just go through from start to finish, and see how you feel. The content inside this book is purposefully layered, meaning you'll discover more each time you read it.

If you can, read it a couple of times in the first week, and aim for at least once a month thereafter. It serves as a beautiful reminder of how elegantly simple and effortless life can really be.

You can also keep the book in your restroom, and randomly flick open and read a section each time you visit. Or store it beside your bed for a little morning inspiration.

The book also makes an ideal gift for friends and family. Add a dash of sunshine to their lives by giving a copy – for no reason except because you love them.

At the end of this book, you'll find the appendices. Take time to explore each section. Appendix #1, "A Short Course in Releasing," goes hand-in-hand with many of the teachings in the 16 rules. Make sure you give it a little special attention.

As a complement to this book, you might also enjoy reading "The 18 Rules of Happiness" (Karl Moore, ISBN 978-0-9559935-1-0).

Well, that's all for now.

So, if you're looking for freedom… If you're wanting to release limiting thoughts and achieve your own happiness… If you're looking for straight-talking self-development…

Read on.

Rule #1:
Stop Feeling
Sorry For
Yourself!

There's absolutely no question about it.

This is my all-time, favorite subject when it comes to the world of self-development. Because if people really *understood* it, they would instantly skip the need for 90% of the self-help courses out there.

I'm talking about SELF-PITY.

Now, let me ask you a question.

How many of us go around feeling sorry for ourselves?

Oh, come on. Admit it. We all do at times. It's entirely natural.

It's fantastic fun to wallow in a little self-pity. Reminding ourselves how terrible the world is. How we've simply *not* been given the opportunities we need. How it's *unfair* that we've lost money, health, friends. How people are just plain *against* us.

We're the victim. And self-pity allows us to give ourselves a little consolatory pat on the back.

Ironically, it actually feels good because we're proving ourselves right in the first place.

"Yes, Karl. You always thought you were worthless. People *said* you weren't, but you knew it really. And look at what happened to you today! Pah! It proves it. You *are* worthless. Oh, what a horrid world!"

See what I mean? *Think* about it.

And it's strange, because most of us don't realize just how *often* we indulge in self-pity. Most of us play the victim over and over again, many dozens of times each day.

We do it when we're moaning about our jobs. When we're worried about our looks. When we're questioning fate. When we're envious. In fact, it's so engrained into our lives, we do it almost automatically.

But self-pity is the very worst emotion. More so than anger, greed or any of the other baddies.

Self-pity eats up everything else around it, leaving only itself standing. It's destructive, it's addictive, it's habitual. And it leaves you feeling powerless.

Yet self-pity also holds the key to eternal happiness – and true self-development, if only you understand it correctly.

You see, if you truly learned to let go of all of your self-pity, then you would be happy. Naturally. Because self-pity is the *only* barrier to happiness.

Or, to put it all a lot simpler:

Stop feeling sorry for yourself – and you will be happy!

Stop moaning about work. Or how crazy your kids are. Or why that person is always rude to you. Or how life, fate, God, is just plain *unfair*.

Yes – life is sometimes cruel. And yes – it may be 100% true that you've been dealt one really crap hand. It's annoying, it's frustrating, it makes you want to weep. There we go.

BUT.

Why bother feeling sorry for yourself?

All it does is zap all of your energy and leave you apathetic. Self-pity may feel good at first – but when emotion dries up, it'll leave you empty and bitter.

So, once again, here it is. The quickest, simplest, easiest, most direct method of changing your life for good. A method that will enable you to instantly become happier, and which will alter the way you view the world forever:

STOP FEELING SORRY FOR YOURSELF.

Stop it. And you will be happy. It's really that simple. There's more self-development in that one sentence alone than almost every self-help course in the world.

So, if you take nothing else from this book, take just that one sentence and make it a part of your everyday life. Every time you feel a tinge of personal sorrow, a flicker of self-pity – just think "Hey, stop feeling sorry for yourself!" – buck up, and get on with it.

The more you do it, the more it'll become part of your personality, the more it'll seriously change your life.

And this simple technique *will* change your life. That's my personal promise to you.

It's a great first step in removing your own inner limitations, and shifting you further toward true freedom, self-development and happiness.

RULE #2:
LEARN TO
LET GO

Letting go is one of the most powerful self-development skills you'll ever learn.

It'll grant you the super-human ability to let go of troublesome emotions at will, enabling you to control your fear, anger, pride and ego – all in one fell swoop.

Now, we all experience emotions every single day.

Emotions are what make us human. And more often than not, they help us. Evolution has selected our basic range of emotions to be the best for our survival.

We experience *grief* after death. We experience *fear* when confronted with danger. We experience *anger* when we're rubbed up the wrong way. These are essential to living.

But sometimes emotions run riot.

They go wild, and lead us into doing things we don't really want to do.

Emotions cause us to *fear* public speaking, our words drying up and our bodies freezing in terror the moment we stand on that platform. Emotions cause us to continue ignoring once good friends, because we're still *angry* at what happened, and can't reach forgiveness. Emotions keep us *yearning* for our addictions to things such as bad relationships or gambling.

So, emotions aren't always good for us. Logically, they don't make sense.

But here's something to remember:

You are not your emotions!

This is a core mistake almost everyone makes.
You *experience* your emotions, yes. But you are *not* your emotions. They're just "feelings" passing through. They're not *you*.

Right? Think about it. You are not your emotions.

And that's not all.

Because emotions are not *you*, you can actually "let go" of unwanted emotions – on demand. You can switch off fear and anger, as easily as you'd switch off a light.

Almost every type of therapy out there has the ultimate goal of helping you to *let go* of your unwanted emotions.

From psychotherapy to tribal screaming therapy, the ultimate goal is the same. To help you let go of the emotions you don't want. To *release*, to let go of your *attachments*. To say "F**k it!" and move on.

But these types of therapy can be a little long-winded. Letting go of emotions *directly* is really the quickest, easiest and most straight-forward personal growth technique.

So, how can you let go of your unwanted emotions?

Well, it can really be as simple as asking yourself the question: "Can I let this go?"

Remember, you are not your emotions. Right now, you're tightly holding onto your emotions without even realizing it. You have a tight clench around *anger* with that annoying person. You have what Buddhists would call an *attachment* to *fear* when it comes to public speaking.

You are actually the one holding on to the emotion. You're in control, and you don't even realize it.

So, make a decision to let go of it. To loosen the clench. To *release*.

Imagine holding onto a small ball, with a really firm grip. So firm in fact, that it's actually hurting you to hold it. But you keep on squeezing it tight. You almost don't *realize* that you can let go.

That's how most of us treat emotions. We don't realize that we can simply let go of the grip… and let the ball fall away.

That's what letting go, or "releasing," is all about.

So, bring to the front of your mind any situation which may have an emotional charge for you right now. A particular person, a frustrating situation, a "mini" addiction. Whatever that may be, and wherever you are at the moment. No need to relax, particularly.

Then, remembering what we've said about emotions, ask yourself: "Can I let this go?"

Answer "Yes" or "No" out loud. It doesn't matter which you answer, just say the first and most natural thing that comes to mind. Both responses are good.

Then, if you can, *feel* yourself unclench the emotion. Allow the tension to be released, and the emotion to roll away if needed. You may wish to breathe out while doing this, or imagine a door in your abdomen opening up. Really *feel* it release.

The process should feel something like when the doctor calls to let you know those worrying tests have come back all clear: a release of tension and anxiety.

If you find yourself resisting, ask yourself: "Can I let this go – just for this moment? Just for now? Just for fun? And just because it's a smart thing to do?"

Again, feel yourself unclenching. Then check how you're feeling. Emotions are like onions: they're layered, and removing one sometimes unveils another. If there's still some charge there, repeat the questioning until you're clear of resistance, or feel like stopping.

This, quite simply, is the basic releasing process.

If you find resistance coming up when you're asking "Can I let this go?" … whether that resistance is anger, fear, lust, greed, passion … then ask yourself: "Can I hold onto this for a little longer?"

If the answer is yes, ask yourself a few more times: "And a little longer still?"

Then either give yourself permission to hold onto it for a little longer. Or, if you decide you've held onto that "bad" emotion for long enough – then just let it go.

Try it out for yourself. Ask "Can I let this go?" with all of your issues and negative emotions. And you may as well do it now. You can let go of emotions at any time – even while mid – conversation in a busy restaurant. No verbalization, special meditation positions or relaxation CDs required.

Also, it's worth noting that this is only a very brief introduction to letting go. As this is such an important topic, I've included a more comprehensive overview – alongside a number of other releasing techniques – in appendix #1, "A Short Course in Releasing."

Master this powerful skill for yourself – and you'll suddenly begin enjoying much more happiness, freedom and emotional control in your life.

Letting go is a true self-development miracle, the real secret behind almost every therapy out there. And now *you* hold the key to unlocking its magic.

RULE #3:
YOUR BRAIN IS
LIMITING YOU

The human brain is a fascinating machine.

The three pound organ contains 100 billion neurons. It can process thoughts at thousands of miles per second. It contains left and right hemispheres, each handling many highly specific functions. Its cortical networks can rewire themselves, effectively remapping how the mind works.

It's amazing.

But here's a thought: maybe the brain is the source of *all* of your limitation.

Bear with me here.

You see, we've already acknowledged that the brain is one powerful computer. In fact, it's universally recognized as being *more* powerful than any computer on earth.

But, ultimately, the brain is really just *that*.

It's a computer.

It records. It plays back. It records. It plays back.

It takes a stimulus, such as a *beach* (or even the word "beach"), and links it with an emotion, such as happiness. In future, when it encounters a beach, it replays the emotion of happiness. Psychologists call this Pattern Matching.

This is great, but it does limit us. Because the brain often relies on its memories and past associations to "relive" the experience – rather than actually just experiencing it in that moment.

It relives the *label* rather than what is actually happening.

Let me give you an example. Have you ever had a stomach cramp – and decided that you were going to be ill? Suddenly, you felt the pains getting worse, and you decided that you needed to go to bed, and your mood worsened. You. Felt. Terrible.

A little later you did a spot check. Perhaps you remembered that you needed to go out somewhere. And you realized suddenly that actually you *didn't* feel quite as bad as you thought. In fact, you didn't feel ill at all. It was entirely in your mind. You were acting as though you were ill, going through the motions – but there were no physical "ill" sensations in your body at all.

That's because the brain had started to play back the "being ill" recording.

You were no longer experiencing what was actually happening in your body, but rather what the label of "ill" in your mind represented.

You were replaying your own *meaning* behind the words.

To prove the power of labels on your brain and body, consider how you feel when you read these words: "Relax… Relax… Relax… Feeling great… So happy, so content, so blissful… Relax."

Or these words: "Tired, tired, tired now… Yawning… Feeling really sleepy… Eyes slowly drooping."

Yawning yet? Try it with negative words too. Go on. Give it a real go for me, right now. See how powerful your own mental Pattern Matching can be?

Get back with me now. *Energetic. Happy. Smiling.*

(Here's a great little test that proves the power of labels in your mind. Visit www.secretartbook.com and signup to receive the MP3 version. We'll also send you the "Colour Name Experiment." It'll amaze you.)

So, we've already determined that our brains – at their most basic functioning level – simply record and playback. Sometimes we don't experience things fully, because our brains are just playing back "faulty" recordings.

We've attached labels to things – and as a result, we're limiting our experience of them.

That's how phobias develop. We watch the movie "Chucky" and suddenly we associate clowns (the stimulus) with fear (the emotion). Suddenly the faintest mention or sight of a clown bring up intense fear within us. Our experiences are limited, flawed. Psychologists call this Faulty Pattern Matching.

So, here's the realization.

Labels are all around us.

In fact, *every single word* is actually just a label.

FEAR. Sadness. Happiness. Foreign. Gay. Pain. Spider.
Jealousy. Muslim. Grief. Fat. Clowns.

They're all associated with things in our mind, every word
causes our brain to hit the "playback" button – rather than
experiencing it for real.

Right?

By letting go of the "meaning" behind the label, by letting go
of our "limiting thoughts" about that label, the recording in
our brain – we can open our eyes a little more, and experience
life a little more authentically.

How do you let go of the labels? How can you stop your brain
"playing back" possibly faulty recordings?

You can't. Labels are still critical. They enable us to function as
communicative human beings.

But if you find yourself hindered by your labels, or feel your
experience is being even slightly limited by them, just sit back
and ask yourself this simple question over and over again,
to *any* thought that arises:

"Is this a limiting thought?"

In other words, is the brain limiting your experience here, with its past interpretation of these labels?

And if it is, because *anything* involving words is, just let it go. (A little like you did in Rule #2.)

Repeat this single question over and over again, releasing over and over on every thought. And because every thought is ultimately a limiting thought, you can let go of everything – and feel your mind instantly become clearer.

This technique gives you a real breakthrough in self understanding. It helps you to realize, as Shakespeare argued, that nothing has meaning besides that which you give it.

And with that realization, you're able to throw away the boundaries that labels have put onto your life so far – and enjoy more happiness in your world.

Yes, the brain is powerful.

But when you also realize that its thoughts are the source of all your limitation, you'll discover a true inner freedom – and enjoy a quantum leap in your own self-development.

Rule #4:
Stop Being
So Damn
Sensitive

You know, there's a high probability that we've never met before.

And yet, I already know quite a bit about you.

I know that you're a highly motivated individual with a strong desire for change. You're probably spiritual, successful, and likely the most energetic and enthusiastic member of your social circle. You're also shockingly intelligent.

Oh, yes. And you're bloody damn sensitive.

You are! You really are! I'm telling you already.

I may have never met you before, but I'm telling you that for a fact. And that's a really great thing, because there are a lot of highly *insensitive* individuals out there in the world. So you're a limited edition.

You have the ability to read people better than most. You're able to take the best steps to ensure the right people are pleased. And you're flexible enough to change and adapt to your environment. You're a social chameleon.

BUT.

In order to achieve true self-development and inner happiness, you must take this next step.

You must let go of wanting approval – and you must stop being so sensitive.

Right now, in simple terms, you spend too much of your time trying to please everyone. You're trying to keep everyone happy, you're hoping the right people like you, you're wishing people approved of your lifestyle. You're being way too damn sensitive about the whole game of life.

And that causes us to become entangled in our emotions. It stops us from living authentically as ourselves and moving forward with our lives.

This section is really a quick practical pep talk to remind you to… STOP!

Have you ever walked into an office – and it instantly quietened? The loud laughs are reduced to a fluttering whisper – and you wonder, you just wonder, what was happening a few moments ago?

Or you're introduced to that beautiful someone at the party – and moments later, they make an excuse and exit the conversation?

Stop being so sensitive.

The office was probably planning your birthday party. And that person at the party likely had a bad case of Delhi Belly.

Your viewpoint is *always* relative. You'll never understand situations from a neutral standpoint, so stop being so sensitive and move on. Or perhaps you've accidentally fallen into the trap of trying to please everyone at the same time?

You're running around like a mad man, trying to ensure that everyone is kept happy. You change your personality to suit each character – and at the end of the day, you're burnt out. Only to start again tomorrow.

Long story short: You cannot please everyone. Full stop. Get over it!

By trying to shape-shift your personality to match the many hundreds of people you encounter each year, you'll not only be left feeling drained, and lacking in self-esteem – you'll also realize that you're living without *authenticity*.

You are not being YOU.

And to be yourself, says Joseph Campbell, is the highest honor anyone is granted.

So, be yourself.

By that, I mean REALLY yourself. The inner self that wants to say "NO!" more often than you do. The inner self that feels proud that it's being genuine, rather than putting on an act. The REAL YOU.

By being more authentic, you'll automatically find yourself surrounded with quality individuals that more closely match your personality. You'll begin enjoying life more, and find yourself more immersed in life's experiences. You'll become real, without any need to hide or change.

And, ironically, people end up liking you more when this side of your personality emerges. By letting go of wanting approval – that desperate, clingy yearning – you automatically gain approval.

So, let's recap this simple and practical rule once again.

Stop being so darn sensitive – and stop wanting approval.

You'll NEVER understand a full situation, so don't let it get to you. You'll NEVER get everyone to like you or your lifestyle, so don't even bother. And you'll NEVER truly understand any other human being on this whole planet, so let them all go jump.

When you place the power of your own approval on something *outside* of yourself, you will NEVER experience true happiness or self-development.

So:

STOP being sensitive. And STOP wanting the approval of others.

And you will experience more happiness, spiritual fulfillment and authenticity in your life.

Rule #5:
Be Happy
Now

We've all heard it about a million times before.

Live in the moment. Seize the day. Be happy NOW.

In fact, I'm willing to bet that you've heard it so many times, it no longer really mean anything anymore. Right?

Let's be honest. If everyone in the world decided to treat each moment as if it were their last, we'd spend our life savings on fast cars, expensive champagne and dubious encounters one day – then regret it all the next.

No. Being happy now is not about extreme living.

But rather it's about making a decision to not put off your happiness until tomorrow.

You know, there's a popular sign in British pubs that reads:

"Free Beer Tomorrow!"

And it always makes me smile. Because, of course, tomorrow never comes.

Most of us spend our time putting off happiness until some future point. Next week, next month, next year. At one point in my life, I spent about seven years working like a dog – and telling myself "Don't worry, I'll be happy next year!"

Of course, next year never came.

Here are a couple of quick home-truths:

Firstly, you might be dead tomorrow. You really might. You might not even make tomorrow. The only thing you know that you have for sure is this very moment. Realize that!

Secondly, you'll die with a TODO list. You won't ever get everything sorted. Accept that and move on. Don't put off your smile just because you're waiting to "finish" everything.

Make the decision to be happy *now*.

Ask yourself: If not now, when?

Let's do a little experiment.

Try to randomly catch yourself at some point today, and check what you're thinking about.

You might be in the past: Thinking about what happened last week, how that person spoke to you, what a great time you had at the party, how embarrassed you were about the wine incident.

You might be in the future: Worried about what you did and how it'll cause you problems, concerned about how the holiday will eventually work out, fretting over future IRS investigations.

But I'm willing to bet that you are NOT in the present.

Your mind will be thinking about anything but now!

You see, we each spend 95% of our time either reconstructing the past or daydreaming about the future. Yet we rarely spend any time actually in this very moment! And our real happiness lies here – in this single moment.

By learning to live more for and in the moment, we become happier people – which is, ultimately, one of the most important goals in the self-development journey.

So, realize to yourself that this moment is all you have. It's the only time you have to change or do *anything*.

In fact: You are only what exists in this moment.

Are you happy right now? Have you been truly living in the moment? What would you change in this moment to make you feel better? Could you follow your bliss even more?

For a moment, join me in a quick exercise. Sit there right now, and consider your thoughts. Try for a moment to get into the *now*.

Let's think about what matters. We only have this moment, we know that. So forget about the past – it's history. It'll never come back and it doesn't matter to us right now. And ignore the future – it's just a fantasy right now.

Think about what *really* matters – this very moment.

Get lost in the moment and discover what's really important. You should find yourself freeing up, opening, feeling more happy and alive. You become more aware of your breathing, your heart, your body.

Gone are your worries of the past. Gone are your fears of the future. Gone are crazy labels, like pain or embarrassment. The only thing which matters is this moment, and how you react to it.

Make a decision to smile, too. Because happiness is *now*!

So, the next time you reach a red light – and suddenly stop singing your favorite song, because nearby drivers are watching – make the decision to be happy now, and continue blasting out that tune!

The next time you decide to save your best clothes and favorite perfume for that elusive rainy day – make the decision to be happy now, and dress smart and smell great!

The more we live for this moment, the happier we become.

Try reminding yourself of this mindset each morning, or whenever you're feeling stressed. It'll help put things back into perspective.

So, stop putting off your happiness until tomorrow – and you'll naturally become a happier person, and take a quantum leap in your self-development journey.

Remember: If not now, when?

Rule #6:
Release Your
Religion

Religion! Now there's a sensitive topic.

But if you're smart enough, you won't be at all offended by what follows. All you need is a genuine desire for freedom – and an open heart.

Let me start by asking a question.

How many of us are limiting our lives, because of the "religion" we have chosen?

It might be an *actual* religion, such as Judaism. It might be the 10-step system from our favorite self-help book. It might be the general belief system of the society in which we live.

We each have our own "religion."

And these religions are holding us back.

They provide a framework to live within. But by default, any framework keeps you packed in.

Does your chosen religion hold you back?

Our religions force us to do things differently. We don't take action, because it's against our religion. We don't follow our bliss, because it's against our religion. We feel unable to change, limited, bound by the system of our religion.

And that stops us from truly experiencing freedom.

So, this section is all about realizing that many of us use our "religions" as an excuse for not taking action. When we realize that, we can learn to disregard the religion – and do it anyway.

This section is about realizing that there are really no rules. It's about releasing our own "religions."

That's freedom.

Let's start with the self-help world.

Now this is an industry littered with redundant religions.

The Secret. Cosmic ordering. Positive thinking. The Law of Attraction. Tarot cards. *What The Bleep.*

These are all systems which tell you how to live. The Law of Attraction has probably received the most focus in recent years. It tells you that similar things are attracted to each other – so think rich, and you'll attract more money into your life.

Some of these things can certainly help guide you toward success.

However they still impose a new set of rules for you to live by, a new religion to follow. You have to make sure you "attract" correctly. You need to follow the precise seven steps for "ordering" from the universe.

When you don't "manifest" the right way – you blame your negative thinking, and beat yourself up. The rules of the religion start to constrain you, and ultimately begin to lead your life.

Right? Think about it.

The truth is that almost 100% of all self-help systems are based on just a couple of core principles. Firstly, you get what you expect. (Rule #7 – Intention Sets Direction.) Secondly, you can let go of "bad" emotions. (Rule #2 – Learn to Let Go.)

But these simple principles are so easy, they aren't attractive enough to most people. So self-development authors surround them in hype and ritual, giving them a seeming importance.

Readers follow these rituals, and limit their experience – by trying to force themselves to follow rules and principles that are simply not important.

Would you prefer to follow the rules of a self-development guru – or would you prefer to be free?

You don't need to follow the crowd when it comes to success and your own freedom.

To experience true freedom, you need to realize that the rules around you can all be dropped. And, if you wish, that includes this one, Rule #6!

The same can be said about the world of real religions – systems that contain more rules than most!

How many people reading this book are currently being restricted by their theistic religion?

They beat themselves up for "sinning." They change their lifestyles to align themselves with their God. They don't mix with certain people because that's what is written.

Let's get one thing straight here: Today, as ever, religions are being used to control people. No doubt about it.

The "rules" are progressively changing, with modern day "leaders" telling the world which bits should and shouldn't be adhered to. The Book of Leviticus tells us we shouldn't eat prawns, but how many Christians or Jews adhere to that these days? How many even know about it?

The rules are fluid. They're not "real." They're not Holy-bound.

And there's no such thing as that mean, evil God sitting and judging you.

(It's worth considering whether there is such a thing as God full stop. Consider reading "The God Delusion" and "The Dawkins Delusion" to make your own mind up. Remember, you can be an atheist *and* spiritually-developed.)

Religions are just a set of rules invented to keep the masses in control. They're a form of police, with the ultimate threat: eternal damnation. Something we can neither prove nor disprove. And so the members of religion continuously live in fear.

Don't.

Decide right now to be free.

Don't let the rules of religion hold you back, or limit your life. I guarantee you'll regret it if you do.

It doesn't matter whether you're Muslim, Christian, Hindu, Buddhist, Jewish, Islamic, or a Scientologist – if you feel limited in any way by your religion, you are NOT experiencing true freedom. If you feel you are sinning, you are NOT experiencing true freedom.

And so.

Every day, people use their religion – from the Law of Attraction to Christianity – to determine how they act. They change their lives to fit the rules. They limit themselves and their actions. And when they get things wrong, they feel bad and punish themselves.

Long story short: Religions restrict you. Release your religion.

And the next time you feel yourself limited by religion in ANY way whatsoever, remind yourself that the real truth is quite simple. Religion forces you to adhere to man-made rules. True freedom doesn't.

So – be free.

Understand this section on a deep level, and you'll have taken a massive jump in your journey toward true self-development.

Rule #7:
Intention Sets
Direction

There's one truly fantastic scene in Alice in Wonderland. It occurs after Alice has shrunk, and she's exploring the dark, mystical forest – desperately attempting to find her way.

Suddenly the disappearing-reappearing Cheshire Cat appears, perched high in a tree. Alice stops and asks him for directions.

"Where are you going?" asks the cat.

"I don't know!" replies Alice.

The cat responds: "Well, if you don't know where you're going, any road will take you there!"

What a revelation.

Do you know where *you're* going?

Let me ask you something. Have you ever been to a party, expecting it to be absolutely great – and it was? And have you ever gone on a night out, expecting it to be truly terrible – and it was?

Perhaps you've got out of bed, stubbed your toe, and decided this was going to be a bad day – and it was? Or maybe you woke up, the sun was shining, and you made the decision that today was going to be fantastic – and it was?

It's funny. You see, we usually get the outcome we expect.

In other words, our intention sets our direction.

It's not that the physical world around us changes. It's just that the way we perceive events alters. It's all in our relative perception.

We notice the good things at the party, and make light of the bad. We soak up the sunshine and smile during a good day, and become a grump on the bad.

We consistently prove ourselves *right*.

So, here's the trick.

By setting a good intention on the things you do, you'll automatically achieve many more positive outcomes!

In fact, this simple principle forms the basis of almost every self-development fad out there.

From *The Secret* to *What The Bleep*, from the Law of Attraction to Cosmic Ordering – and yes, even prayer – they're all based on the idea of laying out a roadmap or goal, and allowing yourself to follow it.

Yet most of these fads build up complicated systems and beliefs to help warrant the price tag. They make the "system" more complex to warrant your purchase of the next book, the next DVD, the next seminar ticket.

But it's really not that difficult.

Distilled, simplified, unwrapped, the concept is the most uncomplicated thing you'll ever encounter.

Quite simply: Intention sets direction. Full stop.

Set your intention – and you'll set your direction.

So, where in your life can you start setting *your* direction?

Try spending a few moments in bed before getting up, deciding that this is going to be a wonderful day. Take a minute before your night out to make the decision that you're going to hook up with some great people. When meeting that annoying business client, set an intention that you're going to get along great and make a real connection today.

It might not work every time, but it'll work more than life *without* intention.

Increase your intention even further. Begin intending positive outcomes during the smallest of exercises. During meetings. During walks. During simple car journeys. During coffee breaks with friends.

Set an intention of happiness and positivity – and watch it come about in your life.

Try it on your mindset, too. Set an intention of being great fun during the party. Set an intention of writing a fantastic novel. Set an intention of being a wonderful parent.

But whatever you do – set an intention.

Henry Ford once said:

"Whether you think you can or you can't, you're probably right."

Think about it.

He was actually saying that whatever we believe will happen, will happen. The things that we hold in mind will ultimately come about. Our intention sets our direction.

This is really one of the ultimate self-development secrets. By applying this, we're setting the compass by which our personal ship sails. It might sound stupidly simple, but it works – and works well.

So, discover it for yourself the easy way. Make setting your intention part of your daily ritual.

Because if you don't know where you're going, any road will take you there.

RULE #8:
SAY YES
MORE

You are fantastic at saying "No."

You really are. You might not even realize it, but you're great at it.

We say "No" to hundreds of things in our lives, every single day.

We say "No!" to our anger. We say "No!" to our lustful urges. We say "No!" to the things we deem to be *wrong*. We say "No!" to change. We say "No!" to criticism against ourselves. In fact, in general, we say "No!" to the world around us.

But you really must get with the latest in self-development fashion.

You see, "Yes!" is the new "No!"

We each spend too much time fighting against the world and what happens within it. We resist what happens in our life. We don't *accept what is*. We say "No!"

Does that sound like you?

The problem is that saying "No!" too much holds us back. It means we spend our time suppressing our emotions and stopping ourselves from moving forward.

When we say "No!" we're swimming against the current. When we say "Yes!" we're swimming with the current.

Which do you think is easiest? Which produces less stress? Which is faster, and more enjoyable?

By saying yes to the world, we instantly become more open and more accepting of everything. Saying yes allows us to accept what's going on, and gives us greater power to change whatever we desire.

So, do you say "No!" too often in your life?

Do you deny your emotions? Do you perhaps try to push down jealousy when it appears? Do you suppress fear? Do you deny lust? Do you desperately attempt to cap your grief?

Try saying "Yes" to every emotion and situation that comes up for you. Accept it. Welcome it. Embrace it. Trust it. Be *okay* with it.

By saying "Yes" to everything that comes up in your life, you enter into a state of flow. You find that life becomes easier, and that you develop a more loving and accepting side.

Remember, saying "Yes" doesn't necessarily mean that you agree with something. If your local neighborhood experiences a spate of violent attacks, saying "Yes" to it doesn't mean you approve of it. Rather, it means you accept the situation – rather than fight against the fact that it's happening.

And that gives you greater power to change it, if you wish to do so. Acknowledgement is the first step on the road to change.

Saying yes more is a ninja weapon in the world of self-development.

It frees you up – and enables you to turn every bad situation into a good situation.

Saying yes more removes your resistance, obliterates your stress, and turns you into a brighter, more lucid individual.

It doesn't just work with emotions either. Saying yes more is also perfect for social situations!

Do you realize just how many times you turn down social invitations? It's possible people don't even ask you out anymore, because they presume you'll say no. And then you complain about how few friends you have. Tsk!

So, when you get asked, say "YES!"

In fact, as an experiment, trying saying yes to everything (within reason!) over the space of a week. That's what Danny Wallace did in his humorous self-help book, "Yes Man."

It changed his life. This simple technique has changed mine too.

By saying YES more, you're giving your life to fate – allowing yourself to be open to the randomness of the world. You're expressing.

By saying NO, you're denying, you're stunting the growth of your own potential. You're suppressing.

So, say "YES!" to the hilarity of life, the next time a bus drives by, splashing into a puddle and soaking your new dress. Embrace your grief, when your pet hamster passes away. Welcome your anger toward that oh-so-annoying situation. Accept all of your own crazy worrying habits.

Say "YES!" to everything.

Literally, *say* it. Say it out loud when things happen. Repeat it to yourself over and over if you wish. It's a great mantra.

So, say YES: Embrace. Welcome. Accept. Drop the resistance.

You know, they say life can only be lived going forward, and only understood looking backward. Maybe that's true for you. Trust that everything has a reason – and say "Yes!" to what happens to you, knowing that it'll make sense in the end.

Let's review.

The Australians call it a "Bias for yes." The Spanish say "Si a todo." Buddhists describe it as flowing with the current of life.

I call it *saying yes more.*

And by saying yes more, you'll become more accepting, more loving, and more in harmony with the world. It's one of the secret tools in your self-development armor – and ultimately gives you more power and control over a situation.

So, if you want to find your freedom, say yes more.

Rule #9: Change Is The Only Constant

Life is a funny old thing.

All around us, every single day, things change.

It's the one thing that moves the whole world forward, and yet as individuals, we consistently resist it. Change is bad. Change frightens us. We do not want change!

But here's a magical little teaching: Everything changes.

It's annoying – but it does.

People die. Kids grow up. Stocks fail. Friends get married. Companies shut down. The things that bring us safety and security alter – and rock our worlds.

This cycle of life, this process of continual change is actually a basic premise in the Buddhist religion. Buddhists appreciate that everything has a beginning, and everything has an end.

It's not just limited to human change, either. Trees, mountains, airplanes, t-shirts, champagne bottles, televisions. Everything has a start point, and everything has an end point.

So when you witness change in progress, you are merely witnessing things passing from one state to another in that journey from beginning to end.

Look around you right now.

Everything around you was created, and everything around you will ultimately be reduced to dust. That includes your body, too. Such is the transience of life. Nothing is forever.

The world is in a constant state of change.

Indeed, the *only* constant is change itself.

At first, this may seem disconcerting. But there's a certain peace in this teaching. Because by understanding what is actually happening, and knowing that this cycle is written in stone, we're no longer "shocked" when these things occur.

Instead, we're able to appreciate the time we had.

Do you fully embrace change in the world right now?

Go and get your favorite household ornament right now. Mine is probably a beautiful grey marble bull that I bought in Mexico. Observe its color, its artistic design, and the workmanship that went into making this wonderful piece of work.

Then imagine it broken, smashed on the floor.

While doing that, try to keep in mind the thought that everything changes. Everything has a beginning and everything has an end.

So, rather than fighting against that transition – with screams, and anger, and weeping – we can instead simply shrug, and understand that's the cycle of life.

Quite simply, everything changes.

So, ask yourself – do YOU resist change in your life?

Are you fighting against the natural cycle from beginning to end?

Think about the last time you really got annoyed at how something changed. Perhaps you lost money in an investment. Or a relationship went sour. Or maybe you crashed your car.

How did you respond?

And can you take a moment out to appreciate how this is all just part of life's constant process of change? How life is churning around everything, constantly?

Just remember that everything is change.

You never step in the same river twice.

Can you even try and *appreciate* more of what you actually have right now – rather than waiting to miss it, once it has left your life?

This process of constant change can also be reassuring in times of need and grief. Because when you find yourself in bad situations, you can always be reminded that the next step in that constant cycle of change is not far away.

Yes, "even this shall pass."

So, don't fight against the constant cycle of change. It happens.

Appreciate the time you have with the things that are important to you – and know that ultimately, everything is reduced to dust.

This is not a cue to be passive toward life, and cease to pursue the positive. But rather, it's a technique for making peace with the world and its many, many inevitable transformations.

Being aware that everything is change gives you an understanding, an awareness… It gives you *perspective* when facing situations we find hard to get our heads around.

Yes, everything changes.

But learning to accept that natural cycle will bring you much greater peace and acceptance – and is worth a million self-development boot camps in your personal journey toward freedom.

RULE #10:
PEOPLE ARE WEIRD.
LOVE THEM FOR IT.

The world would be a wonderful place.

If it wasn't so full of people.

Honestly. It's jam-packed full of them. And whilst they may be the source of one big bag of pleasure, they're also the cause of much of our pain.

This rule is about realizing, on a very deep level, that we'll never really understand any of them – and that we just have to love them for that very reason!

Let's be honest. We all try to be nice and self-developed. And calm. And peaceful. And lovely.

But sometimes you find someone that has the ability to press the wrong buttons within you.

Almost without realizing it, the boiling emotions inside explode into an outrage and you lose your temper. Later, you feel annoyed with yourself – as though you've sinned against the holy doctrine of self-development.

Surely someone that is "self-developed," per se, wouldn't have such an outburst?

Pah. Nothing could be further from the truth.

One of the great lessons in the world of self-development is to realize that, despite Miss Marple's theory, people are in fact all very, very different.

Many people in the world are – let's face it – just *weird*.

They say things they don't mean. They mean things they don't say.

They act in weird ways that just don't make sense. They hide things they shouldn't be embarrassed about. They please people they shouldn't be bothered about pleasing. They remain in relationships that continue to harm them.

They don't listen to sound advice. They are continuously unreliable, unlike your good self. They seem totally unable to keep a single friend. They're socially awkward. They're inhibited in almost every area of their lives. They don't know how to let their hair down.

People are just plain *weird* sometimes.

You're right. Absolutely. I'm on your side.

We understand that.

So, here's the revelation: yes, they're like that. That's life. It's not going to change. People are sometimes weird, fruity screw-ups and you're not going to change it.

Get used to it. And get over it.

You will never find another person on this planet that thinks just like you, so don't bother trying.

If you're searching for that ideal soul mate, don't look for someone who thinks just like you. Firstly, they don't exist, you narcissist. Secondly, wouldn't that all just be a bit boring?

You see, the real teaching here is that yes, everyone is different. We're all weird in some ways. But that's really what makes life, and social interaction, *fun*.

Without the occasion dollop of strangeness, and conflict, and inhibition, and general weird interaction, we'd all forget what it means to be a delicate human being.

So, that's that. We're all different and we're all a bit odd sometimes. Welcome it, and move on.

Here's another thing.

When somebody acts in a particularly strange way, it's easy to get angry. But that doesn't always help the situation. So here's a little trick you can use to become more open and understanding to the way those annoying, know-it-all people behave.

Bring to mind the person annoying you. Try thinking of the moment that person was born, and fast-forwarding through their life to the present. Understand everything that they've been through, everything that has helped transform that blank baby canvas into the individual they are now.

Perhaps a rough childhood gave them a hardened exterior. Maybe a lack of intimacy gave them a social awkwardness. Perhaps a failed romantic life gave them a passion for business success.

If you were in their shoes, and stepped through their life experiences, you'd end up the same way.

Right?

So, fast-forward through their life – and you'll find yourself sympathizing with how they are as people. They are the result of their life's experience. You'd be the same.

Do it for Hitler as an experiment. Even he was merely the result of his life's experiences, the outcome of having gone through life in the way he had. He probably didn't consider himself *evil*.

Think of a person that irks you in life.

Can you give them permission to be the person they are, right now? With their own life, and quirks, and weirdness? And their own distorted quest for happiness?

Can you give them permission to follow their own bliss? Can you even just love them a little more to help them along the way?

Can you fast-forward through their life – and be a little more open to why they operate the way they do?

Try it. It might just help.

And remember that you'll never really understand anyone in this world. We're all a bit strange and kooky sometimes. That's life. It's what makes us individuals.

We may not agree with it, but that's how life works.
Love *them* for being the crazy people they are, and
love *yourself* for being the neurotic individual that you are for worrying about it.

When you truly realize that we're all different, with differing life experiences and motivations, you'll not only open up and be able to connect with others on an even *deeper* level, you'll also become less sensitive and more sociable.

So, be happy, accept these simple facts, and try to love everyone a little more – and you'll be granted one of the true gifts available on the self-development journey.

RULE #11:
YOU CAN'T
CHANGE
THE PAST

We all got history.

No doubt about it.

Every single one of us has a collection of memories and stories that we hold in our minds, and call our "past."

Memories of happy parties and summer days. Of heartfelt reunions and sad partings. Of mundane meetings and sexual encounters.

Each of us has a version of our history stored in our brains – which we each cling to passionately. Our history, you see, makes up what is uniquely us. It's our identity. Without our history, we're a blank canvas.

And there's nothing at all wrong with that approach. History is what makes us *us*.

But sometimes we cling on to painful memories of the past –
and allow them to affect how we act *today*.

We desperately fight against that memory of freezing up when
delivering the wedding speech. Never again will we dare
such a feat. We're fearful when thinking of the time we were
attacked in that darkened alley. Enter stage left, evening street
phobia. We remember those nights of trying to look after our
child, and always feeling like we'd failed. And we're haunted by
that repetitive thought: "Could I have been a better mother?"

Yes. Sometimes our history holds up our future.

So, let's get one thing straight. Let's plainly state one important
self-development teaching.

**You absolutely cannot – under any circumstances
whatsoever – change the past.**

It has gone.

It's done.

It's over.

It's finished.

FULL STOP.

You really need to grasp that concept right now.

You may have made some crappy decisions. You may have
done some bad things. You may have been victimized in some
way, or harmed, or damaged.

But that's the past. It's gone. It's over. You need to move on.

It's also wise to remember that the past is *relative*. It's always from our own perspective – and we never get the full story.

We think our father was distant when we were a child. But we fail to realize he was trying to save a dying marriage, to provide us with a stable family life. It's never quite as cut and dried as we think we remember.

Ironically, the past also tends to change over time.

When we get "hooked" onto a line of thinking, our brain tends to fill in the blanks. We continue thinking about our distant father. Then we remember the time he didn't give us his full support during school sports day. Before you know it, you're sat in a circle with a bunch of self-help addicts, crying your heart out to the beat of an African dream drum.

We tend to forget those times our father was there for us, offering his full love and support. The times he changed your nappy. The times he secretly cried in pride at your accomplishments. The times he worried about you, or did things to help you along your way – without you even realizing it.

Again, the teaching: The past is from our perspective only, and tends to change over time.

It's never as bad as you think you remember.

What do *you* think you remember? Is it possible it could've all been much better? Is it possible that you perhaps don't realize the blessing of that moment?

The problem with our history is simple: some of us just can't let go of it. We clutch to it so tightly, we have no room left to embrace the present. We let it hold us back. We let our "stories" imprison us.

And, to me, that doesn't sound like a smart thing to do.

Are you struggling to move beyond your past? Are you sure you're struggling? I'm willing to bet it's much easier than you think.

Try closing your eyes for a moment and thinking of something from the past. Whatever is on your mind. Think about it, then do the releasing exercise described in Rule #2 "Learn to Let Go"

Ask yourself: "Can I let this go?"

Then stop clutching onto the emotion as you have been doing so far. Release it. Set it free. Drop it. Unclench. Welcome the past, embrace it, accept it.

You must. Because you can do absolutely nothing about it now. And fighting against it will only hold you back in future.

That doesn't mean we shouldn't learn from the past. We should, and must. But we also need to stop the past from holding us back. Try releasing on any anxiety about how our past will affect our future, too.

Remember, the past is a foreign land. They do things differently there. Your past is not your future. Past outcomes are not indicative of future results.

Everything you've done so far in your life has led you to this single moment.

And it is only in this *very moment* that you can change anything.

For it to get you this far, surely whatever happened in your past *cannot* be such a bad thing.

Realizing this can really advance your self-development. It's critical that you realize holding on to the past holds you up in the present.

Memories can be great. But remember this one key understanding: you are *now*, and not *then*.

Release your history.

RULE #12:
FILL YOUR
LIFE WITH
HAPPINESS

You're on a secret mission.

And it might, in fact, be so secret – that even *you* don't realize it's in progress.

You see, everything you do, every action you take, every muscle you move, is all done in an attempt to achieve one single goal. One hidden desire. One state of mind.

Everything you do is in search of... *happiness!*

Think about it.

There is literally *nothing* you do in life that isn't done to make you happier. (Or to avoid pain, which still ultimately makes you happier.)

You slog to work each day, to earn money, to provide for your family and to enjoy a good lifestyle – which makes you happy. You buy flowers for your Mum, so that she approves of you and to express your love – which makes you happy. You go out dancing every Friday night, so that you can find a partner, so that you can get married, so that you can enjoy security – which makes you happy.

Twenty-four hours a day, you are working toward happiness.

Even reading this book, following your own personal quest for self-development and spiritual fulfillment, is ultimately all about being happy.

Yet how many of us make a proactive effort to actually *fill* our lives with happiness?

Subconsciously, we're working toward it all the time. We don't realize what we're doing. But by working on it *consciously*, we can make massive steps toward being happier – and ultimately become a brighter, smilier, more self-developed individual.

Actively surrounding yourself with happiness is a fantastic step forward in your self-development journey – and often replaces the need for a million self-development remedies.

So, how can you fill your life with happiness?

Well, start with music.

Music has a profound effect on your mood. It's been scientifically proven that listening to upbeat music can seriously boost your state of mind.

So fuel your iPod with your favorite happy tunes. Create a morning mix CD to get you out of bed and smiling away. Play smooth upbeat jazz while you work to rocket your productivity. Go book yourself in to watch a musical or pantomime.

Surround yourself with positive, happy music – and just watch the difference in your life. (See Appendix 5 for happy music suggestions.)

What else?

Well, have you tried dancing recently?

Dancing is the number one activity for increasing the presence of feel-good chemicals, such as serotonin, in your brain.

Not only does dancing make you happier, it also improves social interaction skills, provides a little much-needed touch-therapy, sharpens your co-ordination, and keeps you super-fit!

I'd highly recommend trying out salsa dancing for a great start to the dancing world. You don't have to be an expert to get started, and it can truly change your life.

Next up is being grateful.

Because I'm willing to bet that you really *don't* count your blessings every day.

Do you?

Taking a few minutes out each day just to be really *grateful* for all the wonderful things you have in your life has been *proven* to make you happier. That's right – they actually did scientific tests on this and it's a *fact*.

And no matter what you think, even in your most depressed of moods, you've *always* got something to be grateful about.

Give thanks for your family, your friends, your children, your partner. Be grateful for your health, your legs, your heart. Appreciate your emotions, your hope, your happiness, your desires. Really thank your experience, your quest for change, the air you breathe.

You've *always* got something to be grateful for. So be grateful – and be happier.

How about loving more, too? *Giving* love is known to make you happy. So try loving more in your life. Give love to people easily – even to those you don't think deserve it. It really does come back ten-fold.

Try being more social, too.

Research has found one thing in common with the happiest and richest of people. They all have large social circles. How big is your group of friends? When was the last time you tried to proactively expand it?

Increase your network of friends, and you'll discover a whole new level of happiness in your life.

And it doesn't stop there.

Try doing good things for no reason at all. Practice what the world calls "*Random Acts of Kindness*" – just because it's a nice thing to do. It'll make you feel better about yourself, without a shadow of a doubt, and you'll be helping to spread a little of your joy.

Appreciate the pleasure to be found in your simple routines. That morning cup of coffee. The evening stroll in the park. That friendly chat at the bakers. Take real enjoyment in life's little gifts, and setup routines that you can enjoy in future.

Also, try spending your money on *experiences*, rather than on material goods. It's been proven that experiences provide lasting memories, worldly exposure, and boost your happiness for longer than physical purchases. When the new Mercedes is full of dog hairs, or your new iPhone has been scratched, the thrill of the physical has soon gone. So, *experience* – don't hoard.

Think about what makes you smile – and do more of it.

Yes, it sounds simple, but how many of us do it? Try considering what really drives you, what you're passionate about, and fill your life with more. Joseph Campbell put it more succinctly: "Follow your bliss." Are you following yours?

You know, there are too many "self-developed" people in this world that walk around without smiles.

They are really "above" happiness, and spend their days meditating, their minds floating somewhere outside our happy human world.

Don't be one of them.

Surround yourself with happiness – and you will have taken one of the biggest ever steps to finding your freedom.

RULE #13:
BE A RICH
MONK!

The self-development world is a wonderful place.

But it's full of crazy misconceptions. Silly ideas about things that you *must do* or *must experience* in order to become truly self-realized.

This section is about realizing that these firm ideas are really nothing more than urban myths. It'll help you stop getting caught up in your own limited thoughts – and speed you down the freedom freeway.

To get started, let me tell you about a friend I have in London called Jin.

Now Jin is on the self-development journey. He's a seeker. He's looking for something.

Speaking to me just last week, he bemoaned: "I can't believe it. I've tried everything and nothing works. I've just left a month-long self-development workshop in the States – and I still don't *feel* right. I've simply not had that big bang moment yet!"

Whoah. Crazy Misconception #1 In Progress.

You do not need an epiphany in order to enjoy freedom
and the results of self-development. You do not need to be
dramatically healed, or see an angel, or feel just *so* different.

Many people in the self-development are waiting – as Jin put it
– for that *big bang*. Until that occurs, they don't feel *fixed*.

Drop the foolishness. You don't need – and probably won't get
– an epiphany. Get over it, and be free as you are right now.

Which leads us on to Crazy Misconception #2: You can't
be *fixed*, because you aren't *broken*.

Many individuals that enter the world of self-development feel
bad or wrong or poisoned in some way. They feel they've been
broken – and that they need to be fixed.

Well, you are not broken. You're already whole and perfect
as you are right now. There's absolutely nothing you need to
change. You're only feeling limited by the limiting thoughts
you hold in mind.

So stop trying to *fix* yourself. You are not *broken*.

Moving on to Crazy Misconception #3: Spiritual people give
up their possessions.

Uhm. Sorry?

Many people in the world have the misguided belief that in
order to be fully realized, they must give up their worldly
goods. They consider gifting their home to a Buddhist retreat

and spending the rest of their lives meditating in a remote wooden hut.

Well, realize that it doesn't have to be that way.

You can be 100% spiritual and self-developed and free – while still living and operating in the modern world. It's the way of the cosmopolitan self-developed warrior.

The idea that you shouldn't have both cash *and* spiritual fulfillment is both antiquated and just plain *wrong*.

We all know that money can't buy you happiness. But it can certainly make things much easier.

So, be a living example of breaking that urban myth – and be a rich monk.

And that takes us to Crazy Misconception #4: You must meditate in order to be self-realized.

No way!

This is one of those crazy ideas perpetuated by hardcore Sedona residents that want nothing more but to sit in a circle and "Ohm" all day long. Personally, I indulge in some meditation – but getting my mind into a near lifeless state is something I'd prefer to reserve for when I'm dead.

If you want to meditate, then meditate. If you don't, then don't.

There's absolutely no reason you *must* meditate in order to truly discover your own freedom.

(If you're interested in meditation, I heartily recommend the Brain Evolution System as an 'advanced' meditation program. It's based on scientific brainwave research, and you can learn more at www.brainev.com.)

So, let's quickly review.

You don't need an epiphany. You're not broken. You don't need to throw away all of your money. You don't have to meditate. And this is just the beginning.

Think about your life right now.

What other rules, myths, superstitions, are you allowing to be imposed on your thinking?

What other things are you telling yourself that you *must* do in order to get where you're going?

What other rituals are you undertaking, just because others say that's what *should* be done?

Where are the beliefs you're subscribing to right now? And have you questioned them recently?

Do you avoid walking under ladders? Do you get nervous saying "Beetlejuice" thrice? Do you get worried about detail after swearing on somebody's life?

Perhaps you're even a little nervous about this rule... Rule #13.

Drop the weird beliefs. They don't serve you.

Release, and set yourself free of your self-created prison.

Stop following the crazy rules, follow your bliss, and you'll be a self-developed, spiritually fulfilled, rich monk. And a better person for it.

RULE #14:
SADNESS IS OKAY.
IT'S ALL GOOD.

Our glorious world is absolutely crammed full of *opposites*.

In order to have *dark*, you must have *light*. In order to have *up*, there must exist *down*. In order to have *love*, the world must also have *hate*.

In fact, these are not so much opposites as *pairs*.

They give meaning to each other. Without one, the other cannot exist. We must experience the "bad" in order to truly appreciate the "good."

That makes sense.

Right?

**Yet how many of us try to cram our lives
with *happiness* – and completely reject the *sadness*?**

How many of us attempt to fill our minds with *positivity* – and beat ourselves up the moment we start feeling *negative*?

We know that both sides are essential to life, and that one cannot exist without the other. Yet we continuously try to push down sadness and negativity – rejecting it, ignoring the fact that it even exists.

Does that sound like you at all?

Are you trying to hold onto just one side of the coin?

Do you find yourself desperately trying to resist sadness and negativity in your life?

What other pairs are you not fully embracing?

When things come up in pairs like this, we say they *arise in duality*. And in order to truly appreciate life and its experiences – and to enjoy true freedom – we must learn to fully embrace the duality in everything, starting with happiness.

To do this, simply ask yourself the question:

Can you welcome the *happiness*? And can you welcome the *sadness*?

Welcoming doesn't mean that you *want* sadness, or that you accept the "wrong parts" of duality. It just means that you *accept* it. You recognize the emotion – and rather than fighting against the emotion itself, you just let it be.

Other replacements for "welcome" here are: *accept, embrace, release, let go, let it be.*

Ask yourself this question and take time to feel the answer. Repeat this process over and over, releasing on any charges you have surrounding how those pairs make you feel. *Feel* yourself letting go. Take as long or as short as you need. Actual *releasing* can happen instantly, and you may never have a problem with that duality again.

(To learn more about releasing, remember to read Rule #2, and Appendix 1: "A Short Course in Releasing.")

Once you've released on the happiness/sadness duality, move on to other pairings:

Can you welcome the *positivity*? And can you welcome the *negativity*?

Can you welcome the *good*? And can you welcome the *bad*?

Just keep asking yourself the pair of questions over and over, and answer to yourself honestly. And it's okay to say "No." You'll let go of troublesome emotions regardless.

You can even try using this process on any other issue that stirs up resistance inside yourself. Just ask: "Can I welcome ABC? And can I welcome the opposite of ABC?"

Repeat that over and over, until you feel like stopping, or feel that you've released the resistance around that issue.

This concept of accepting the duality is an essential part of the Buddhist teaching.

That's why the taijitu (yin-yang) symbol looks as it does. Think about it. The symbol shows apparent "opposites"

– black and white – intertwined. Within each side is also a dot of the opposite.

Yet these opposites are actually reliant on each other to make a whole circle. They depend and support each other. And the dots represent that within each side is a small part of the opposite, and a potential for change.

The symbol reminds Buddhists to embrace the duality in everything, and that change is forever possible.

My hope for this section is to simply provide a reminder to you that we can never *only* embrace the positive, the happy, the joy. Sometimes we must also embrace the negative, the sadness, the tears. It exists, and it cannot be ignored.

So, when it crops up in your life – embrace it with both arms, experience it, and watch it neutralize away regardless. And one way to do that is using the duality exercise above.

Life is full of peaks and troughs.

You don't know when you've hit a peak until you're coming down. And you don't know when you're in a trough until you're climbing out.

To bring meaning to an all-too-common phrase: It's all good.

If you want the rainbow, you've got to put up with the rain.

By realizing this, you'll naturally embrace everything much more willingly, your life will become less stressful, and you will have taken another massive step toward true freedom and self-development.

RULE #15:
YOU ARE NOT
YOUR STORY

For thousands of years, human beings have been wonderful *story tellers*.

There's a built-in yearning to get sucked into a story, to get lost in the drama of the moment, to orate and share your own tales with the world.

Modern story tellers include movie producers and politicians, actors and artists, mothers and fathers. As a society, we respect and admire great story tellers. It's the reason films and television has become so immensely popular. They tell *stories*.

We each love our own stories, too.

I have a wonderful ghost story about a house I once lived in, which gets spookier and more intricate every time I tell it. It's guaranteed to make your hairs stand on end, and I revel in a chance to tell it.

But by far and away our most common types of story are the stories about *ourselves*.

We're great at sport. We're pretty good at karaoke, but get nervous if singing in front of family. We love tomatoes, but they really need to be cored – or they make us feel a bit sick. We keep falling back into abusive relationships, no matter how hard we try not to.

These are our own "mini-stories." And often, they're harmless enough.

It's when our stories start to hold us back that they become an issue…

"My name is Janet – and I'm an alcoholic."

"I'm Jason – and I'm a failed father, and drug addict."

"Yes, I'm Patrick – and I'm a homosexual with intimacy problems."

Sometimes, our stories restrict us.

They define us as a very particular type of person, and ensure that we're kept locked in our own self-created prison. Our stories *pigeon-hole* us.

Not only that, we also build on them – much like I do with my ghost story. We make them bigger and badder with each telling. We give the stories more power. Soon, our original stories become irrelevant – and our new stories take on a life of their own.

They eventually start to lead us, cripple us.

We carry the weight of our stories around with us each day. They stop us from achieving true freedom, they limit us to working a particular way – and yet we continue holding onto them.

To use an Eastern term, our stories are our *attachments*.

However, not everyone lives like this.

Those that enjoy true freedom, individuals that are genuinely self-developed, know this simple fact:

You are not your story.

You're not!

Whatever amazing story you can tell about your terrible past, how you've always failed time and time again, how life has dealt you an unfair hand, how things were just plain wrong, how you can't break the addiction – you are still NOT your story.

Past results are not indicative of future performance. What you were is not what you are.

It's just what *happened to you*. It's not YOU.

You are not your story. You are not your emotions. You are not your past.

And if you could just learn to let go of your story – you'd instantly release all of your baggage, and you could start today the way that you would like. Without limitation. Without issues. Without *attachments*. Without unwanted stories.

To some degree, our stories provide us with comfort. It's the devil you know. The sick safety blanket. They enable us to indulge in self-pity, and enjoy a little sympathetic attention. But it's pointless holding on to the story, because it's limiting you today.

So, make a decision right now to be the change you wish to see you in your life.

Let me repeat that, because it's exceptionally important:

Right now, make the decision to *be* the change you wish to see it your life.

Sit back and think of the stories you have formed about your life. All those great stories you have about how your marriage started falling apart in the early days, and how you've been rescuing it ever since. Great stories about the time you were bullied, and how it made you feel suicidal. Fantastic stories about how life sometimes *stinks*. Especially yours.

Think about one of *your* stories.

Then ask yourself: "Can I let this story go?"

Can I drop this story? (Even if it's a good one?) Can I release this story? Can I unclench the tight fist I have around this story? Can I let go of desperately holding on to it, and making it part of "me"?

And, if you can, just do it. Let go. Breathe out – and release. Feel it drop away. (See Rule #2.)

Don't go into it. Don't try to analyze the details. Don't dig around to figure out the "hidden lesson." Just ask yourself if you can drop the story. And if you can, do it.

Because your story, really, is ultimately just that. A *story*.

People cling to stories because they think they give their life meaning.

Incorrect.

Life doesn't have meaning.

The meaning of life is the meaning you bring *to* life.

What meaning would you like *your* life to have?

Make a decision to shape your *own* story, starting today – and you'll discover a true freedom and happiness uncovering itself in your own wonderful life.

RULE #16:
SMILE, LAUGH,
LOVE YOURSELF!

❦

Some years ago, I decided to take the introductory class at a local Buddhist retreat.

After much waiting, the Chief Guru serenely glided into the room, his bearded face lacking all emotion. He sat on the stool in front of the class, and slowly pieced together his words.

"What makes us happy?" he asked.

"My new trainers," answered the guy next to me. The Chief Guru told him he was wrong, and gave all the reasons why trainers didn't make you truly happy. This event was clearly not sponsored by Nike.

He continued for a further two hours explaining why physical things couldn't make us happy. He conveyed the idea that, yes, indeed, happiness comes from inside.

Much head-nodding and sycophantic clucking later, everyone left. They'd all been fully instructed on the *true* meaning of happiness by Chief Guru – and were in awe of his wisdom.

But here's the thing.

During the whole experience, not a single person either *laughed* or *smiled*.

Nobody! Not the Chief Guru. Not the people attending the class.

Is that the kind of true self-enlightenment you'd like to experience?

This rule is a reminder that you should make a decision to be *happy*. Regardless of what others tell you, what others do, or what's happening in the world around you.

You see, being happy is the ultimate goal of true self-development.

Those that aren't happy, aren't truly self-developed.

Learn to be happy with what you are, and what you have.

If you aren't happy with what you are, you won't be happy with what you'll become. If you aren't happy with what you have, you won't be happy with what you get.

So, make a pact with yourself right now to be *happy*.

Part of that is deciding to smile more. Deciding to love more. Deciding to laugh more. Deciding to love *yourself* more.

These things will each make you a happier person.

Because, let's admit it, you'll never be 100% self-developed. No way, José.

We're all a little bit screwed up in one way or another.

We're pedantic about the strangest of things. We have little quirks that other people find kooky. We obsess over detail, or beat ourselves up over the craziest of things.

Right?

Just for once, why don't you *congratulate* yourself on how great you are at making a mountain out of a molehill?

Why don't you give yourself a pat on the *back* for focusing on issues and "problems" that aren't really important?

Why don't you say well *done* to yourself for being so good at holding onto issues from your past?

Let's be honest: You're great at it! You do it better than anybody else!

You're flawed.

You're perfect.

So, smile, laugh, and love yourself for being the wonderful crazy person you are – and you'll take the greatest self-development step ever.

Ever wondered why the Dalai Lama laughs so much?

My belief is that he's recognized the hilarity of life, with all of its ups and downs, with all of earth's many inhabitants worrying about their small, crazy, funny little problems.

He's "zoomed out," and sees how adorable we all are. He sees the happiness behind our apparent veil of problems and issues.

So, again – make that decision to beat the crowd.

Smile, laugh, love yourself.

And you will achieve enlightenment.

The Secret Art Of Self-Development Review

Rule #1 – Stop Feeling Sorry for Yourself!

Self-pity is the worst kind of emotion. It turns you into a powerless victim. So make a decision to stop feeling sorry for yourself now – and take a massive leap in your self-development.

Rule #2 – Learn to Let Go

We're each clutching to our emotions, causing ourselves pain and stress. By letting go of emotions, we experience greater freedom. You are not your emotions. Just ask yourself: "Can I let this go?"

Rule #3 – Your Brain is Limiting You

The brain is simply a powerful computer. It records and plays back. It uses "labels" such as sadness and illness to replay things in your mind. Drop the labels. Ask yourself: "Is this a limiting thought?"

Rule #4 – Stop Being So Damn Sensitive

This rule is simple: Stop being so sensitive, stop wanting approval, and stop trying to please everybody. By being your authentic self, you'll automatically become more real and likeable.

Rule #5 – Be Happy Now!

We spend most of our time either dwelling on the past, or fantasizing about the future. Try to take time to actually live in the *Now* – and enjoy real freedom. You are only what exists in this moment.

Rule #6 – Release Your Religion!

We each have "religions" holding us back in the world. From Judaism to the Law of Attraction. Every belief system simply adds a new set of rules to your life. Release your religion, and embrace freedom.

Rule #7 – Intention Sets Direction

We usually get the outcome we expect. So, set an intention in everything you do – from going to a party to your first day at a new job. Set a positive intention, and prepare for a positive outcome

Rule #8 – Say Yes More

We each say "No" to too many things in our lives. Try saying "Yes!" to emotions, situations, invitations, and see how your life changes. Flow with the stream of life, and it all becomes easier.

Rule #9 – Change Is the Only Constant

Everything changes: people die, kids grow up, companies shut down. Rather than fight against the cycle of life, embrace it – and realize that absolutely everything moves on. Even this shall pass.

Rule #10 – People Are Weird, Love Them For It

Some people are just plain kooky. Get used to it. Try quickly fast-forwarding through that person's life to sympathize with their motives. But realize this: you'll never truly understand anybody.

Rule #11 – You Can't Change the Past

Sounds obvious, but we all try to do it. Realize that what happened in the past is over. Stop wasting energy visiting past events in your mind. Move forward from this moment onward.

Rule #12 – Fill Your Life with Happiness!

Everything you do is in search of happiness. So, fill your life with happy things: surround yourself with happy music, take a dance class, be grateful, expand your social circle, enjoy more experiences.

Rule #13 – Be a Rich Monk!

Get rid of your crazy misconceptions. You don't need an epiphany to be self-developed. You're not broken, so you can't be fixed. You don't need to meditate or give up your possessions to be spiritual.

Rule #14 – Sadness is Okay. It's All Good

In order to experience happiness, we *must* experience sadness. When sadness arises, embrace it – and watch it dissolve. If you want the rainbow, you've got to put up with the rain.

Rule #15 – You Are Not Your Story

Don't get wrapped up in your story. Stories restrict and cripple us. Past results are not indicative of future performance. Let go of your story – and enjoy true freedom in the now.

Rule #16 – Smile, Laugh, Love Yourself

Make a decision to be self-developed and *happy*. We're all a little screwed-up. Love yourself for being crazy and pedantic. Laugh more at the wonder of life. And smile, because you're free.

CONCLUSION

Self-development is indeed an honorable journey.

It's the desire to find your own freedom. It's the wish for happiness. It's something that most people spend a lifetime seeking, and no time finding.

You, however, are ahead of the game.

You've absorbed the sixteen powerful "rules" inside this book.

You've taken on board what is means to "Find Your Freedom" (Lester Levenson) or to "Follow Your Bliss" (Joseph Campbell) or even to "Let Go And Live in the Now" (Guy Finley).

You've come to realize that you are the result of your own thoughts.

You've realized that you're only limited by the thoughts you hold in your mind. And that you can be happy simply by making a decision.

You've decided to stop feeling sorry for yourself, to let go more, to stop being so sensitive, to be happy in his moment, to release your religion, to set your intention daily, to say yes more, and to embrace change.

You've made a decision to love the crazy people around you, to stop trying to change the past, to fill your life with happiness, to let go of "labels," to embrace both happiness and sadness, to appreciate that you are not your story, and to smile more.

You've made a decision to indulge in *real* self-development. And a result, you've found both a greater freedom – and a profound inner happiness.

You're now a finder – and no longer a seeker.

Take the time out to read this book a few more times, if you can. Really immerse yourself in the sixteen rules, and apply them to your life. You'll be surprised at the difference they make.

Thank you. Know that I'm proud of you.

Here's to your freedom!

Wishing you much love and happiness,

Karl Moore
www.karlmoore.com

APPENDICES

Appendix 1:
A Short Course
In Releasing

Releasing is a fantastic tool for unleashing freedom in your life!

It allows you to let go of sadness and limitation, and embrace freedom and happiness. It enables you to drop negative emotion and increase positive emotion.

Releasing allows you to control your feelings, rather than letting your feelings control you.

In fact, I'd consider releasing to be perhaps the most important self-development technique on the planet.

Sound interesting? Well, let's start from the beginning.

Emotions are how we *feel*.

We feel *grief* after the death of a family member. We feel *anger* when somebody rubs us up the wrong way. We feel *pride* when we do a great job.

Emotions are useful, and help make us human.

But sometimes emotions hold us back.

They cause us to freeze in *fear* when about to deliver our speech. They cause us to continue being *angry* toward someone we should've forgiven long ago. They cause us to carry on being *addicted* to gambling, or bad relationships.

Yes, emotions have a lot to answer for!

But the good thing is that you can control your emotions just as simply as you'd control a light switch. Turning them off is as simple as *<click>*.

You see, the secret you must realize is this:

You are not your emotions.

That's right. You are not your emotions. And your emotions are not you.

Emotions are just things that you *experience*.

Rather than "I am angry," a more accurate description might be "I am experiencing anger."

And rather than "I am courageous," a more precise version may be "I am feeling courageous."

So, emotions are just things you experience. Sometimes they feel good, sometimes they run riot. And you can switch them off as easily as you'd switch off a plug socket.

How?

Through the process of *releasing*.

Now, releasing is all about letting go of your negative emotions. When you let go of negative emotions, you'll feel lighter and more stress-free. You'll enjoy greater freedom and feel more at peace with the world.

Releasing is always a great idea.

(You can let go of positive emotions too, and you'll typically feel even more positive as a result.)

How can you release?

Firstly, you need to recognize that we're each desperately holding onto our emotions – even those emotions that aren't serving us. We're clenching them, like we'd clench our hands around a pencil or a small ball.

We're holding on to that *fear*, that *grief*, that *apathy* – because we somehow think that it is *us*, and that we *need* it.

But when we realize that we are not our emotions, and that we don't need a particular emotion, we can simply choose to let it go.

That is, we can unclench our fist – and allow that emotion to simply be free, or even drop out of our hands altogether.

Let's try it together.

Think of something right now that you know is a concern for you. It might be a situation at work, or a particular person you dislike, or just some general worry that you have. Make it a simple issue for now, just for starters.

Think of that thing, and notice the resistance that builds up in your stomach.

Then simply ask yourself the question:

"Can I let this go?"

Which is another way of saying: Can you unclench the grip you have around this feeling right now? Can you release the grip? Can you let go of the resistance? Can you just drop the *emotion* attached to this issue?

As you ask yourself "Can I let this go?" – breathe out, and answer honestly with "Yes" or "No" out loud. It doesn't matter which you answer with, it'll all provide you with an emotional release on some level.

While exhaling, *feel* the release happening. Feel yourself unclenching that grip. Feel yourself just letting go of that emotion. Notice the difference?

Remember, *we* are the ones that are holding on to our emotions. We are the ones that are causing them to continue living inside our minds.

Would you prefer to hold on to your negative emotions even more, allowing them to bubble away inside your mind – or would you prefer to just let them go?

Remember, by letting go, we're not agreeing with it, or letting somebody off the hook. We're simply releasing the *emotion* attached to it. We're granting *ourselves* greater peace and serenity.

Then, when you're ready, connect to see whether that issue still has any charge.

If it does, repeat the process once more: connect with the issue, ask yourself "Can I let this go?", answer "Yes" or "No" while breathing out, and *feel* the release.

Loop on this entire process a few more times.

You'll soon begin to really *feel* very different about the whole issue.

Within minutes, you'll notice the emotion has drastically reduced in size – and may just have disappeared altogether. Right?

Finished? How did that feel?

Let's try it once more. This time, make sure you follow through the entire process. Out loud, too, if you can.

Again, think of a situation which brings up some resistance in your tummy. It might be an annoying person, or a small worry that you have right now.

Get in touch with that sensation, that energy, that feeling. Then ask yourself:

"Can I let this go?"

Answer the question out loud, with a "Yes" or "No," while breathing out. Remember, any answer is fine, they both work the same magic. Just be honest.

As you answer, loosen your clutch on the emotion. Relax into the comfort. Release.

Feel yourself unclenching. Feel yourself *letting go*.

Releasing feels great. It's like the feeling you get when the doctors call you, after those worrying tests – and say you've got the all clear. It's total relief. That's releasing.

To help you feel the release even further, imagine two doors in front of your stomach opening, allowing all of the negative emotion just to flow out – as you let go. Really *feel* it happening. Great!

Finished?

Now check how you feel.

If there's still any emotional charge left, no worries. That's fine! Repeat the process until you feel better about the issue, or want to finish.

If you don't feel any progress at all, don't worry either. Just let go of trying to get results. Sometimes you're too busy "watching" to really experience.

And if you answer "No" during the process and don't feel yourself able to let go, don't worry about that either. Every step, no matter how redundant it may feel, helps take you closer to emotional freedom. Just release on it and move on.

And that's it, really.

Releasing is the quickest and easiest method for letting go of troublesome emotions.

It's the hidden process behind almost every therapy out there – from psychotherapy to tribal drum therapy. Except here we're just releasing the emotions directly, rather than fluffing up the process.

There's no need to spend years sitting on a couch, going into your "back story" and analyzing precisely *why* things happened that way. Here, we just release directly – and move on.

It really is as simple as that.

Just connect with the emotion and ask yourself: "Can I let this go?" – then breathe out, answer "Yes" or "No," and *feel* yourself letting go.

Easy!

FURTHER
RELEASING METHODS

There are other ways of releasing, too – all based on the same core "letting go" principle.

One of the most popular is the *three questions* method.

This was popularized by the late Lester Levenson, and is now taught in the Abundance Course (www.releasetechnique.com) and The Sedona Method (www.sedona.com).

This technique is based on the following premises:

1. We *don't know* that we can let emotions go

2. We *don't want* to let go of emotions

3. We always *put off* letting go until later

So, this method of releasing works by addressing each of these questions – allowing us to cycle through, and slowly let go of the emotions that are holding us back.

Here are the steps:

1. Think of the situation, and connect with the emotion you'd like to release.

2. Ask yourself: "*Could* I let this go?" (yes/no – answer out loud, honestly)

3. Move on to ask: "*Would* I let this go?" (again, yes/no)

4. And then: "*When?*" (now/later)

5. Feel that release – then check to see how the situation feels. If there's still some emotional charge, go back to step one and loop again: you'll find some issues are layered like onions, and are released over multiple passes. Or if you feel stuck in the actual process itself, let go of "*wanting* to feel stuck," and start again – or rest for a while.

Another popular releasing method is the welcoming technique, popularized by many releasing teachers, including

Chris Payne with his Effort-Free Life System (www.effortfree. com).

Here are the steps to follow for this technique:

1. Lower your head and place your hand on your chest or stomach. Get in touch with an emotion, or a situation that has an emotional charge for you.

2. Notice the intensity of the feeling in your body, and rate the intensity from 0 to 10.

3. *Welcome* the emotion, much as you'd welcome a friend into your home. Welcoming doesn't mean you agree or forgive the emotion, just embrace it, accept it, welcome it. Allow it to be there, instead of pretending it doesn't exist. *Feel* the welcoming.

4. Now get in touch with the emotion again. How does it feel?5. Rate the intensity again, from 0 to 10. Keep going until it comes down to 0. If you feel stuck, ask yourself if you could let go of trying to *change* being stuck – or simply continue later.

Releasing teacher Lester Levenson (whose work is now continued through The Abundance Course and The Sedona Method) also used to suggest that individuals try letting go of wanting *control*, *approval* and *security* too. These are general terms that can help you release on emotions right across the board.

You know, releasing is all about letting go of emotions. It's about detachment.

It's what the Eastern world calls letting go of our *attachments* and *aversions*.

In the Western world, this releasing process is essentially the equivalent of saying:

"F**k it!"

(A wonderful argument set forth by John C. Parkin in his book of the same name.)

Try each of these techniques yourself, and start using whichever suits you best. But remember to *try* them.

Releasing isn't just for reading about. It's *experiential*.

CONCLUSION

Releasing is a powerful method for gaining greater emotional freedom.

It helps you realize that you are not your emotions – and thereby allows you to release all of the limiting thoughts, emotions and feelings that have held you back in the past.

You'll become happier, enjoy more self-empowerment, and simply be *more free* when you discover releasing for yourself.

Take time out to go through all of your issues, negative emotions, and the people in your life – releasing on each in turn. You'll feel the benefits immediately.

Just keep asking yourself "Can I let this go?"

Practice it as often as you can – and do it all the time. Even when you're talking to somebody, you can release there and then, in that moment. It's simple and it's easy.

To learn more about releasing, I'd suggest one of the following books:

- The Sedona Method – by Hale Dwoskin – www.sedona.com

- The Abundance Course – by Larry Crane – www.releasetechnique.com

- The Secret of Letting Go – by Guy Finley – www.guyfinley.com

- Effort-Free Life System – by Chris Payne – www.effortfree.com

- F**k It – by John C. Parkin – www.thefuckitway.com

Discover releasing for yourself, embrace it in your daily life and I promise you'll never look back.

Even if that releasing is as simple as saying "F**k it!" just a little more often.

APPENDIX 2: QUOTES TO INSPIRE

Life has a habit of throwing crazy situations our way, giving us chance to demonstrate our character in the way we handle them.

But one thing's for sure, we're never the first person in that situation. The whole plethora of human emotion has been experienced googol times by a billion other people.

And that's why quotes are great.

They help us to connect with other people's wisdom, and to learn from our cumulative experiences of life.

That's why this section contains some of my favorite ever quotes – to help inspire you during the times you need it.

A ship is safe in harbor... But that's not what ships were built for – *William Shed*

There is nothing either good or bad... But thinking makes it so – *William Shakespeare*

All that we are is the result of what we have thought. The mind is everything. What we think, we become – *Buddha*

The cave you most fear to enter contains the greatest treasure – *Joseph Campbell*

Life is not measured by its length, but by its depth – *Anonymous*

If you can imagine it, you can achieve it. If you can dream it, you can become it – *William A. Ward*

Life is without meaning. You bring the meaning to it. The meaning of life is whatever you ascribe it to be. Being alive is the meaning – *Joseph Campbell*

There is one quality which one must possess to win, and that is definiteness of purpose, the knowledge of what one wants, and a burning desire to possess it – *Napoleon Hill*

The people who get on in this world are the people who get up and look for the circumstances they want and if they can't find them, make them – *George Bernard Shaw*

The pessimist sees difficulty in every opportunity. The optimist sees the opportunity in every difficulty – *Winston Churchill*

Put yourself in a state of mind where you say to yourself, 'Here is an opportunity for me to celebrate like never before, my own power, my own ability to get myself to do whatever is necessary' – *Martin Luther King, Jr.*

We are what we think. All that we are arises with our thoughts. With our thoughts, we make the world – *Buddha*

I try to learn from the past, but I plan for the future by focusing exclusively on the present. That's where the fun is – *Donald Trump*

I can't change the direction of the wind, but I can adjust my sails to always reach my destination – *Jimmy Dean*

I want to sing like the birds sing, not worrying about who hears or what they think – *Rumi*

The highest reward for a person's toil is not what they get for it, but what they become by it – *John Ruskin*

Men are born to succeed, not to fail – *Henry David Thoreau*

I figured that if I said it enough, I would convince the world that I really was the greatest – *Muhammad Ali*

Happiness is not having what you want. It is wanting what you have – *Unknown*

Success is getting what you want. Happiness is wanting what you get – *Dale Carnegie*

The talent for being happy is appreciating and liking what you have, instead of what you don't have – *Woody Allen*

When you come to a fork in the road, take it – *Yogi Berra*

Fortune favours the bold – *Virgil*

He who lives in harmony with himself lives in harmony with the universe – *Marcus Aurelius*

If you haven't got charity in your heart, you have the worst kind of heart trouble – *Bob Hope*

It is not length of life, but depth of life – *Ralph Waldo Emerson*

Everything that happens happens as it should, and if you observe carefully, you will find this to be so – *Marcus Aurelius*

Act as if it were impossible to fail – *Dorothea Brande*

If you do not conquer self, you will be conquered by self – *Napoleon Hill*

Nobody can go back and start a new beginning, but anyone can start today and make a new ending. – *Maria Robinson*

The future depends on what we do in the present – *Mahatma Gandhi*

Dream as if you'll live forever, live as if you'll die today – *James Dean*

Attain to the place where no one and no thing can disturb you – *Lester Levenson*

When one door of happiness closes, another opens, but often we look so long at the closed door that we do not see the one that has been opened for us – *Helen Keller*

In the hopes of reaching the moon men fail to see the flowers that blossom at their feet – *Albert Schweitzer*

All the world's a stage, And the men and women merely players. They have their exits and their entrances; And one man in his time plays many parts – *William Shakespeare*

If you do not change direction, you may end up where you're heading – *Lao Tzu*

History will be kind to me for I intend to write it
– *Winston Churchill*

APPENDIX 3: EXPERIENCES TO OPEN YOUR EYES AGAIN!

Every now and then we all get stuck in the routine of life.

We need something to open our eyes to its wonder again.

This section is all about that. It provides a handful of suggestions that you can use to bring a little child-like magic back into your life.

So, randomly pick something from this list – and get to it, right away!

- Make a list of six things you could do this evening. Then roll a dice and let fate decide!

- Find somebody else on the Internet with the same name as you, get in touch and try to make a new friend

- Visit Wikipedia and click the "Random Article" link on the left hand-side. Get lost in the site for an hour, discovering worlds you never knew existed. If the article talks about a place nearby, drive there

- Decide to say "Yes!" to everything for a month, a week, or even just for a night. See what doors open for you!

- Open an atlas, close your eyes, and randomly stab your finger anywhere on the page. Decide to go there for your next vacation

- Join an Internet dating site, and remember what it feels like to flirt a little!

- Lookup and hook up with a few old friends from school.

- Find them at Friends Reunited, Classmates.com, or on Facebook

- Buy an item of food from the supermarket you would never usually purchase. Indulge!

- Send a random "Hello!" text message to the person with the mobile/cell number one digit up and down from you

- Get to know your neighbors

- Decide to "play" today. Go to the seaside, enjoy a little bowling, play a board-game with family!

- Be mischievous. Play a prank and don't worry about getting caught!

- Enjoy a leisurely meal with your loved ones … share the preparation of the meal … enjoy the time together

- Celebrate your loved ones by creating a family journal of photos, notes and special memories

- Spend time walking in an inspiring natural location with a friend you haven't seen for a while. Enjoy conversing with your friend – listen to their insights and share some of yours

- Go for a 20 minute power walk to clear your mind, boost your circulation and improve your energy levels

- Buy 12 life-changing books and read one a month

- Try a completely new activity – something you haven't done before and enjoy the adventure of learning something new

- Sit under a tree for an hour or three and just do nothing. Listen to the sound of nature's voice. Enjoy the stillness of being in the moment

- Do something nice for someone you don't know. And do it anonymously. Your feel-good factor will soar as a result of your kindness.

- Join a dance class. Go wild, have fun and enjoy the freedom of moving to the music. Try a local Five Rhythms class if you prefer spiritual over disco or salsa

- Spend a night star-gazing. You cannot fail to be awe – inspired by the magical, vast universe that is out there

- Rekindle old friendships … spend a day catching up and enjoying the company of old friends

- Go out to the nearest city with the intention of making one new friend. Strike up random conversations, visit coffee shops and libraries, and see where the day takes you

- Be creative: take a pottery class; learn how to paint with oils; try basket-weaving

- Do something spontaneous, and for no reason at all

- Go visit a nearby comedy club

APPENDIX 4:
FOODS TO MAKE
YOU HAPPY

A nutritious, balanced diet is the key to good health and longevity. But did you know that some foods actually enhance mood and help maintain those all-important feel – good vibes?

Eating for happiness – as well as health – should be your primary goal. To obtain the sustenance you need, include the following foods in your diet:

- **Foods high in Omega 3 – ie, oily fish, nuts, flax seeds.** Omega 3 has been scientifically proven to reduce depression and increase happiness. Try also taking a daily supplement, too

- **Foods rich in tryptophan – ie, lobster, turkey, pineapple, tofu, bananas.** Tryptophan is converted by the body into the feel-good chemical serotonin, which increases your well-being

- **Foods with plenty of amino-acids – ie, chicken, turkey, fish, cheese, cottage cheese,** eggs, milk, nuts, pulses, bananas, avocados, wheat germ, and legumes. These foods help maintain correct amino acid levels, essential in balancing your mood

- **Foods which raise vitamin B levels – ie, spinach, peas, orange juice, wheat germ or avocado**. Solid vitamin B levels help safeguard yourself against depression

Also:

- **Whole grains such as oats, quinoa or brown rice** contain B vitamins to ensure the slow release of sugars needed to maintain well-being

- **Carbohydrates, such as cereals, rice, pasta and starchy vegetables** provide slow energy release to maintain a balanced metabolism

- **Regular 'energy snacks' such as fruit, cereal, seeds and nuts** help maintain energy levels and good mood throughout the day

- **Pomegranates, goji berries, blueberries, raspberries, avocados, mangoes, apples, macadamia nuts, spirulina, broccoli and spinach** – all super-foods that contribute to overall wellness

And remember these feel-good food pointers:

- Vitamins and minerals – especially the B vitamins – are essential for correct functioning of the nervous system and help to prevent illness linked to depression, anxiety or dementia. Vitamin D supplements have been shown to help with Seasonal Affective Disorder (SAD). Always take a good multi-vitamin and mineral supplement

- Ditch adrenalin-fuelling coffee and choose relaxing herbal and fruit teas to aid tranquility and boost well-being. Also drink a few glasses of water each day to maintain correct hydration

- Eat fresh, organic foods where possible. Choose raw veggie or fruit options

- Replace junk foods (high sugar / high salt / high fat / high additives content) with natural foods – vegetables, fruit, grains and seeds

- Always eat in moderation

- Believe in the healing properties of the food you're eating

- Enjoy your food! Hang up your worries and frustrations before you sit down for dinner. When you think calm and happy thoughts while you're eating, it will aid your digestion and ensure that the food provides you with the energy and healing needed

Treat your body well. It's the only one you have.

Good nutrition is essential to maintain optimum state of mind, body and spirit. What you choose to eat makes a real difference, so choose the perfect ingredients for a happy you!

For more information on how food can affect your mood, alongside ideal meal plans for your mind, visit www.foodandmood.org.

APPENDIX 5:
SONGS TO MAKE
YOU SMILE

Most of us forget just how much music affects our mood!

So, find out what music makes you happy, and surround yourself with it. Load it onto your iPhone, create a mix CD for your car, play it on your computer at work.

And if you're unsure what makes you happy, here are a few fantastic suggestions to get you started!

Fascination – *Alphabeat*

Wake Up Boo! – *Boo Radleys* (Proven in scientific studies to be the 'happiest song in the world!')

She Moves in Her Own Way – *The Kooks*

Love Train – *The O'Jays*

The Voice of Truth – *Casting Crowns*

Shiny Happy People – *REM*

I'm Working My Way Back to You Babe – *The Spinners*

Sunshine, Lollipops & Rainbows – *Lesley Gore*

Search For The Hero – *Heather Small: M People*

Don't Worry Be Happy – *Jimmy Cliff* or *Bobby McFerrin*

What A Wonderful World – *Louis Armstrong*

We Are The Champions – *Queen*

Simply The Best – *Tina Turner*

If You Want to Sing Out – *Cat Stevens*

I Had The Time Of My Life – *Bill Medley & Jennifer Warne*

My Way – *Frank Sinatra*

Greatest Love Of All – *Whitney Houston*

You've Got A Friend – *Carole King*

All You Need Is Love – *The Beatles*

Ray Of Light – *Madonna*

Headstart For Happiness – *The Style Council*

I Can See Clearly Now – *Jimmy Cliff, Johnny Nash* or *Bob Marley*

We Will Rock You – *Queen*

Wind Beneath My Wings – *Bette Midler* or *Colleen Hewitt*

O Happy Day – *Sister Act*

Paint The Sky With Stars – *Enya*

Orinoco Flow – *Enya*

Good Morning Starshine – *Serena Ryder*

Walking On Sunshine – *Katrina and The Waves*

I Believe I Can Fly – *R. Kelly*

Chariots Of Fire – *Vangelis*

Return To Innocence – *Enigma*

I Feel Good – *James Brown*

Beautiful Day – *U2*

New Day – *Celine Dion*

Eye Of The Tiger – *Survivor*

O Fortuna – *Carmina Burana by Carl Orff*

Nessun Dorma – *from Puccini's opera Turandot*

Lovely Day – *Bill Withers*

The Roses Of Success – *Chitty Chitty Bang Bang soundtrack*

Rocky Theme Tune

Appendix 6:
Claim Your Free
MP3 Version Of
This Book!

Do you learn better by *listening*, rather than reading?

Don't have time to read the full 16 rules right now?

No problem. We've created an MP3 version of this entire book for you to download – so that you can listen whenever you get a spare few minutes.

On your computer, on your iPod, or in your car!

To download your copy, simply visit www.thesecretart.com.

You may be required to answer a security question before being given the download link.

You can also buy the official audio CD version of this book – "The Secret Art of Self-Development" – online at Amazon.com.

Enjoy!

CPSIA information can be obtained
at www.ICGtesting.com
Printed in the USA
BVOW09s0227261017
498611BV00001B/128/P